# FAMILY
# GARDENS

# FAMILY
# GARDENS

**Bunny Guinness**

David & Charles

To my children, Unity and Freddie

A DAVID & CHARLES BOOK

First published in the UK in 1996
Reprinted 2004

Distributed in North America
by F&W Publications, Inc.
4700 East Galbraith Road
Cincinnati, OH 45236
1-800-289-0963

A catalogue record for this book is available from the British Library.

ISBN 0 7153 0924 2

Please Note: Great care has been taken to ensure that the information contained in this book is
both accurate and complete. However, since the skills and competence of individuals vary
widely, and no book of this nature can replace specialist advice in appropriate cases, neither the
author nor the publisher can accept legal responsibility or liability for any loss or damage caused
by reliance upon the accuracy of such information.

Art Editor **Lisa Tai**
Photography **Juliette Wade**
Illustrations **Kevin Hart**

Printed in China by SNP Leefung
for David & Charles
Brunel House      Newton Abbot      Devon

Visit our website at www.davidandcharles.co.uk

David & Charles books are available from all good bookshops; alternatively you can contact our
Orderline on (0)1626 334555 or write to us at FREEPOST EX2110, David & Charles Direct,
Newton Abbot, TQ12 4ZZ (no stamp required UK mainland).

# Contents

# Introduction

The final nudge that propelled me into action on this book was my son's fourth birthday party. We had organized a clown to entertain the children's friends and as it was a sunny day we decided that the fun and games could take place in our small back garden. As we settled back into our chairs, looking forward to some gentle amusement, chaos erupted around us. The clown, who normally has all onlookers spellbound, was totally ignored – indeed, no one even seemed aware of his presence. All the children were immersed (some literally) in the attractions of the water garden – reeds, frogs, fish, dragonflies, snails, pebbles and sludge. After an hour of trying to attract attention away from this wildlife extravaganza the poor entertainer gave up, muttering, 'There is just no way anyone could compete with that.'

Of course he was right. An enticing garden can offer children a vast amount of scope for thrills, spills and excitement, far more than the confines of orchestrated entertainment, no matter how good. But how often do you see gardens that are planned around the whole family? We seem to veer between extremes: either the whole garden becomes merely an area to contain plastic climbing frames and the like which make any attempt to create an attractive garden impossible, or else any hint of family fun is banished, sacrificed to the cause of a garden that is purely for admiring.

Now that people tend to be more established in their own homes before their first child comes on the scene there has usually been time to make the best use of all the space, inside and out. It seems a shame to go back to square one with the garden and banish all thoughts of aesthetic values

once the family begins to grow. This precious outdoor area may be the only safe space available where children can play without a watchful adult breathing down their neck, and they spend thousands of hours here with their parents, siblings and friends. Yet most families spend fewer hours, less thought and far less money on fulfilling the potential of their garden than they do on indoor toys and videos, many of which become discarded all too quickly.

I have aimed to describe in this book how to design and create a garden which will have elements to inspire everyone, from hyperactive ball players to green-fingered artists. I have tried to stress how important it is to get the whole family involved, so that everyone has a vested interest in the garden. After all, every member of the family must have one part of it that strikes a chord, be it only the position of the hammock!

*Make sure that all the family have a say in the development of the garden – even small children will enjoy selecting flower and vegetable seeds from catalogues, books or garden centres and helping to decide where to plant them. Encourage children to plant up their own small patches of ground in their favourite parts of the garden.*

# DESIGN
# AND
# PLANNING

*No garden can be a real success unless the overall*

*design is right. This is particularly true of the family*

*garden, which must cater for both children and adults*

*with radically different ideas about the purpose of the*

*plot of land outside the door. At the same time the*

*garden must look good while requiring no more*

*maintenance than you are comfortably able to provide.*

*It is often not feasible to create the whole garden at*

*once, but as long as you have a cohesive plan at the*

*outset, the work may be carried out in stages.*

# Enjoying your Garden

Adults generally have a good idea about what they want from their garden — whether it be a beautiful, tranquil oasis where eating and entertaining can take place outside, or a plantsman's paradise. However, most adults also appreciate that what children want from a garden is equally important and essential to harmonious family life. This book will show how your child's desire to climb trees, make dens, ride bicycles and kick balls need not conflict with your own garden dreams.

### COMMON MISTAKES

It is all too easy to concentrate time and money on home improvements, but to neglect the many options offered by a garden. When children start pulling the heads off prize blooms and finding other undesirable methods of amusing themselves outside, a few items such as a tubular climbing frame and a plastic sand pit may be set hastily in the middle of the lawn. The garden is dramatically changed and its development halts until the children are older. This book will show how to bring adventure, exhilaration and mystery into a garden for children without forfeiting its character and charm for adults.

### MAKING THE MOST OF A GARDEN

Even without climbing apparatus, ball games and sand pits, the garden environment has much to offer children. It appeals to all the senses with bright colours, exotic perfumes, interesting sounds, tactile plants and plenty to taste in the vegetable garden. An added bonus is that a garden is continually changing. Exciting events happen every day: sunflowers bloom, birds hatch, dandelion clocks scatter, frog spawn arrives and bumble bees feed from foxgloves.

However, for a family to make the most of these natural pleasures, a garden must be well-designed. The garden is usually larger than any room in the house and even in a small garden, each family member should aim to have their own private space. It is here that children will create a fantasy play world away from prying eyes while adults find peace in the potager or potting shed. There should also be areas which encourage the family to come together; a terrace, pool or seating area could all provide this opportunity. If the garden is well-planned, life can be idyllic with children happily and constructively occupied outside from dawn to dusk.

*This jungle-like mass of bamboo and other plants provide a tranquil hide-away for reading and dreaming. These sorts of spaces offer so much more scope for play and adventure compared to the more static and sterile world of an indoor playroom.*

*An old stone sink provides an outdoor place for water play and for cleaning vegetables and hands before they hit the kitchen. It provides an ideal work-and-play area which is also used for sailing toy boats.*

### THE VALUE OF OUTDOOR PLAY

Toddlers and young children discover new things every day. They are developing their senses and learning physical skills, usually by touching, tasting, testing, grasping and climbing, or simply observing everything in their world. Adventures of this sort must often be discouraged in an indoor play area where space is limited and precious things hard to repair. In the garden, however, safe areas can be created to allow children to develop vital skills and give full rein to their desire for investigation. Sand pits let children weigh, mix, pour, taste and tunnel, while a safe water feature gives them a continual source of absorbing interest not only from splashing about, but also through watching wildlife.

## PLAY STRUCTURES IN THE GARDEN

A playhouse or tree house is the child's domain, where they can 'live' in the manner they most enjoy, find some privacy and escape from the confines of the house. Climbing and swinging structures, dens, pets and various games can all be far better accommodated outside, and they can be designed to blend in well with the garden.

## CHILDREN AND GARDENING

A creative way to harness children's energy is to encourage them to garden. Spend time gardening with them, letting them do the choice bits, giving them seeds that are easy to grow and bedding plants on the point of flowering. Or why not help them plant a wigwam of willows that they can water and train (*see pages 40-1*).

Partly because so many things are new to children and partly because they have not yet developed long concentration spans, they will attack projects only in short bursts initially. Recognize their short attention span and make gardening fairly action-packed so as to arouse and develop their enthusiasm. As they become more interested do not be surprised to discover a mini vegetable plot or palatial pool for a family of newts has found a place in your back garden.

## A TRUE FAMILY GARDEN

A private garden is fast becoming the only outdoor space in which children can play safely without constant adult supervision. Involve

*In this town garden, tough but interesting planting flanks a well-used lawn. A raised walkway and 'flying fox' (cable runway) link up with a tree house leaving the lawn area open enough for ball games while maximizing the play potential.*

children in each stage of the garden's development. Leaf through gardening books together to whet their appetites, take them to other gardens, parks and wild areas and see which 'habitats' are appreciated most. Encourage them to draw sketches of tree houses, paddling pools and climbing trees, and make use of these whenever it is practical, so that they feel they have contributed to the garden's development and you feel that you are fulfilling some of their dreams.

# The Changing Garden

Whether you are making changes to an existing garden, or creating a new garden from scratch, the cardinal rules, to my mind, are a) to set out an overall plan before you start to make any alterations b) to tackle the improvements over a comparatively long period of time (such as ten years or more) and c) to retain an element of flexibility so that the garden grows with you.

With an overall master plan you can ensure that all the elements of your garden will eventually complement one another. For example, if the plan has an area designated as a conservatory but you do not yet have the funds to build one, in the meantime, make sure that the garden surrounding that area will fit in beautifully when your conservatory is in place.

### WHICH GARDEN FEATURES?

To arrive at the overall master plan, each member of the family should decide what they would ideally like to have in their garden. Once this list is built up it will probably need to be edited until it matches what is possible in terms of space and budget. Adults and children are likely to have different preferences (*see chart*).

### RESOURCEFUL PLANNING

Few people are lucky enough to have both the space and money for everything they would like in the garden, but think again before excluding features which you think are unachievable. If you crave a woodland garden, much can be achieved in a small space. If you have, for example, a 3m (9ft) wide strip of land along a boundary, careful selection and close planting of young, inexpensive 60–90cm (2–3ft) tall trees will produce a woodland

### ADULTS' REQUIREMENTS
- Sheltered eating and entertaining area
- Barbecue
- Tranquil place in which to relax
- Water feature
- A screen from neighbours
- Kitchen garden area with vegetables
- Garden room for office or studio
- Shed for storage
- Greenhouse to allow plant propagation
- Lawn
- Woodland area
- Orchard
- Herb garden
- Pergola
- Japanese garden
- Herbaceous borders
- Area for pets/chickens
- Private place to sunbathe

### CHILDREN'S REQUIREMENTS
- Playhouse or den
- Space to pitch a tent
- Climbing frame
- Tree house
- Sandpit
- Paddling pool
- Wildlife pool
- Area of long grass for stalking games
- Place to ride bikes
- Woodland for games and privacy
- Stream or bogland ditch for games
- Flowering borders which attract bees and butterflies
- Pet area
- Vegetable or flower plot
- Area for ball games
- Swimming pool
- Swing
- Trees for climbing

edge habitat easily within ten years. It will be an attractive natural play space, a wonderful backdrop to the garden – perhaps hiding a neighbouring eyesore – and a delightful wildlife habitat.

### ADAPTABLE PLAY FEATURES

Some garden play features can easily be converted to another use once the children are grown up. With a modern butyl liner, sand pits can quickly be converted into ornamental or wildlife pools. A climbing structure can be designed to function as a pergola at a later date (*see page 64*), and climbing plants provided they are sited sensibly can be grown around the structure from day one. As parents become grandparents, a summer house can be adapted so that it also functions as a playhouse – perhaps by fitting a small door inside the adults' door, like a judas gate. A tree house might start off near to the ground for young children and be extended with ladders and ever higher storeys as the children grow.

*TOP LEFT This climbing structure of rustic poles is an ideal feature for a family garden combining interest for the children with an attractive appearance.*

*TOP CENTRE Children love water and this paddling stream, constructed from granite setts, is drainable and when empty looks like an edging channel to the terrace. Designed and constructed by Roger Storr.*

*TOP RIGHT This small playhouse is perched on top of a boundary fence and has been built by two neighbouring families for their children to share, with access from both gardens.*

*BELOW LEFT Swinging tyres (available from play equipment manufacturers) can be added to trees and structures to give good play value, simply and inexpensively.*

*BELOW CENTRE Children find animal sculpture particularly appealing, and it is worth considering siting some near to the areas of the garden they use.*

*BELOW RIGHT This den was made by pulling the trunks of young trees together at the top and weaving branches in between them. As the trees grow they will probably fuse together and form a living tree house which changes from year to year.*

# The Master Plan

To make a successful master plan, you must bear a number of elements in mind: the needs of adults and children, the amount of maintenance you can provide, the requirements of wildlife and, of course, visual appeal. Different areas of the garden will have different functions and therefore different characters, creating interest and contrast, yet they must add up to a unified whole.

### EMPHASIZING THE BEST FEATURES

Make sure that you have highlighted all the advantages of your garden (fine views, changes in level, natural water, charming old fruit trees and so on) and have come to grips with its problems (lack of privacy, lack of shelter, ugly views of your own or your neighbour's house). Think about all the pluses and minuses and mark them up on an overall layout of the garden. Designing a scheme is often easier when you have problems because the design develops naturally as a means of solving them.

The house is often the most dominant feature in a garden, but unfortunately few are chocolate-box visions of loveliness. The first thing to do is to make a critical appraisal of your house's good and bad features. These will be most obvious in the dead season, and if you are planning your garden in summer it is a good idea to resort to photographs taken in winter if you have some. As you are going to be continually viewing your house from the garden, you want to direct the eye to its best features and mask out eyesores such as a bleak gable end or a botched-up lean-to with planting. Very ordinary houses can be transformed by clever garden design, so make this aspect a top priority.

### KEEPING IN CHARACTER

It can be quite a challenge to incorporate all the elements you want into a cohesive design. Unless the area is very small, you will probably have to break the garden up into different spaces by means of fences, planting, pergolas, hedges, paving or levels. Try to decide what feel or character you want to create in each space, and how they will flow into each other. Once you have decided on the character for a particular area, follow through in all the details. For instance, if you want a cottage-garden feel, choose plants such as fragrant old roses, foxgloves and delphiniums and avoid conifers and hybrid tea roses; use hedges, old walls or willow hurdles rather than larchlap panels as boundaries. If you are searching for styles to emulate, the best way is to visit other gardens and to look through books.

*ABOVE This is the garden building where Roald Dahl used to write. The pleached limes which flank the approach dramatically alter the overall impression of the structure, enhancing its appearance as well as serving to link it with the garden. Make your planting work equally effectively around your buildings, masking less attractive features and emphasizing the best ones.*

*LEFT Areas of mixed planting create a soft, lush, vibrant feel. Try to plant some of them so that they are accessible for children and adults by means of a network of narrow, informal paths and tough plants. These intimate spaces exude a secret, secluded character equally conducive to quiet contemplation or imaginative play.*

*A Town Garden*

This garden belongs to a family with six children, the majority of whom are in their teens. They all enjoy the games lawn, where the net is used for badminton, deck tennis and volleyball. The paved eating area is conveniently sited outside the French windows to the kitchen, enabling the family to eat al fresco without fuss or extra work, and at the far end a wildlife area with a pool and garden building provides a peaceful hideaway.

**KEY**

Gravel with plants

Mixed border

Flowering meadow

Mown grass

Hedges

N

*TOP This garden is divided into three different levels. In the upper one there is a generous paved area adjacent to the house with this simple swing hanging from the spectacular weeping ash tree just off centre. CENTRE The middle level is a simple, well-balanced lawn area enclosed by attractive boundaries on all sides. Views down to the wilder area and up to the terrace and house heighten the interest. BOTTOM On the bottom level a mown path bordered by a wilder area leads to this charming thatched building the far side of the small pool. The hut was built and thatched by the owner — a first attempt with the aid of a DIY book from the library.*

LEFT *Before you start to make alterations to your garden, check that you have fully appreciated the potential of all the existing features. Old fruit trees may be non-productive but they may still have the capacity to accommodate highly prized assets such as swings, dens, ladders and tree houses very successfully.*

A paved area is often adjacent to the house, so its design must be complementary to the building – an old stone farmhouse would be sadly spoiled by a sea of modern red brick paving around it, for example. Do not make this paved area too small as it will probably be well-used and also highly visible from the house. Try to avoid the use of just one type of material, which can look bleak; instead break up the paving with patterns and planting.

### BREAKING IT UP INTO AREAS

Deciding which features to put where will usually require a bit of juggling, as there are often many different options. Logic may dictate certain things such as putting an informal pool in an existing depression in the garden, a herb garden near the back door or a woodland screen to hide a tower block, enabling some elements to fall into the best place fairly easily. Others will no doubt cause

a few headaches. If you can designate a separate area for children, make it a slightly private and wilder place where you can camouflage some of their activities with tough tree and shrub planting. This will act as a magnet for them, concentrating their more robust efforts away from your more delicate designs.

If you have the space, do include an area of lawn which can be used by all the family, sometimes perhaps for ball games which can be enjoyed by everyone. However, try not to surround it with your most prizeworthy borders, and use tougher plants on the edges. The alternative is to limit ball games to the periods when herbaceous plants are dormant.

The water feature is another aspect that everyone will find attractive. While there may be a small depression just right for it, it is perhaps most important to site it where it can be easily appreciated from the house so you can watch the visitors it attracts.

Providing an area for growing vegetables and herbs is a worthwhile use of space. Do not feel you have to banish these useful plants to the less visible extremes of the plot; consider putting them near the kitchen door and laying out a series of small, easy-to-tackle beds in an attractive pattern, divided by narrow paths. Add a few attractive elements – a seat, some clay seakale forcers, some runner bean wigwams, a raised sink in which to wash the produce, a few terracotta pots stuffed with herbs, some sunflowers, nasturtiums and sweet peas – and then no doubt you'll all end up wanting to sit in it.

When you think you have arrived at an overall layout for the garden, mark the design out on the ground with canes and string and live with the anticipated alterations in this form for a while to make sure that they will function in the way you hope; it can be a mistake to bring in the bulldozers straight away.

### A Country Garden

*This sloping garden is divided into a series of different rooms by retaining walls and hedges. The wilder area away from the house is used regularly by visiting grandchildren to make dens and play chase and ball games. The long upper terrace forms an ideal eating and entertaining area which has views out over the garden. A yew hedge screens the view of the cars in the driveway.*

*BELOW In this area of paving edged with a retaining wall the lavish planting is visually the dominant element. The generous expanse of hard surface looks good all year round.*

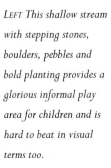

N

*LEFT This shallow stream with stepping stones, boulders, pebbles and bold planting provides a glorious informal play area for children and is hard to beat in visual terms too.*

*RIGHT Here, areas of different character are separated by different levels. This is the view from the middle terrace over the lower terrace and through the archway to the wilder area.*

**KEY**

 Mixed border

 Flowering meadow

 Mounding

 Play structures

 Willow tepee

 Archway over bench

# Disguising Utilities

Most family gardens have their fair share of eyesores including telegraph poles, compost heaps, rabbit hutches, greenhouses, water butts, carports, parking spaces, manhole covers and oil tanks. Particularly in a small garden, where space is very precious, a good solution is to build these utilitarian features into an attractive design from the outset. A compost heap (*below left*) has a yellow brick wall behind it with handsome detailing and decoration, a rabbit hutch can be a pleasing lawn feature (*see page 144*) and sheds and carports can be built to blend in with the garden.

### SCREENING EYESORES

A different approach is to screen the problem. A garden shed might be sited at the bottom of the garden, totally concealed under a mass of ivy. Telegraph poles may be screened by growing trees in the foreground. Oil tanks become less obtrusive if they are painted in a garden-toning dark finish and hidden away behind hedging or a climber-covered trellis.

### PLANNING PARKING AREAS

Cars and car-parking spaces need careful planning. Clever detailing of the paving to provide a footpath up to the house, flanked by gravel parking spaces either side, will give the appearance of an attractive front courtyard when empty (*see opposite*). Light trellis structures covered with climbers, are also attractive and effective ways to screen and shade cars (or indeed caravans), making them less intrusive in the garden.

### CONCEALING MANHOLE COVERS

Manhole covers often crop up in unwelcome places. If you are lucky enough to choose where they should go, try and incorporate them in a border or path. They become eyesores when their siting looks haphazard. In borders, plants can be grown over them to screen them, and in paths they can be totally concealed by using recessed covers topped by matching paving.

### IDEAS FOR SHEDS

Before opting for a purpose built shed which you will probably want to screen, it may make sense to design and build your own version which satisfies a need for storage but also complements the garden (*see below right*).

### STORING TOOLS

If you do not have space for a shed, choose well-designed tools and hang them high near the back door, ready for action.

OPPOSITE LEFT *In a small garden it is well worth making facilities such as compost heaps look good, maximizing on every square inch of your plot. The sun motif was hand-made from clay, while the well detailed brick wall behind forms an attractive but functional backing. Designed and built by Roger Storr.*

OPPOSITE CENTRE *This rustic screen is interesting, provides an ideal support for climbers and at the same time shifts the eye away from the dustbin area behind it. Designed and built by Roger Storr.*

OPPOSITE RIGHT *This garden building is of a basic but clever design. It forms a covered eating area during the summer months when the canvas blind is rolled up, and in the winter when the blinds are kept down against the weather it is used to store firewood. Designed by Landscape Architect, Honor Gibbs.*

TOP LEFT *Two families, both with young children of a similar age, live in adjoining town gardens and the children frequently want to play together. This stile-cum-ladder forms an ideal solution providing easy access with no loss of privacy.*

TOP RIGHT *This looks totally unlike a carport, and yet is one. The gravel defines where the cars go and the paving slabs take you to the door. Abundant well-designed and maintained planting show the house off at its best. Designed and constructed by Sheila and Roger Storr.*

BELOW RIGHT *Most gardens have a shed, and more often than not they are better tucked away. Here, you can hardly spot this useful storage space hidden away behind a well-managed jungle.*

# A Modern Town Garden

WHEN SPACE IS LIMITED SOME OF THE MORE PRACTICAL ITEMS OF GARDEN LIVING, LIKE MANUFACTURED PADDLING POOLS, GARDEN SHEDS AND RABBIT HUTCHES NEED CAREUL SITING. THIS DESIGN OFFERS SOLUTIONS FOR HIDING THE NEGATIVE AND ACCENTUATING THE POSITIVE IN A GARDEN.

Although designed to be of interest to the whole family, this garden is particularly geared towards the young children as the time they spent in the garden heavily outweighed that spent by their parents.

### THE PLAY AREA

The garden is very open and visible from much of the house so the play area is tucked behind a dense evergreen hedge. This allows the children to play in privacy while being sufficiently close to the house to allow some degree of supervision. It also keeps plastic play equipment out of view from the house and terrace.

A variable width of vigorous planting surrounds two sides of this area, forming a buffer zone of tough shrubs, such as willow, bamboo and buddleia in which the children can play. Plants such as foxgloves, ox-eye daisies and verbascum self-seed freely, providing dots of colour. At one end of the play area, a large climbing frame is well sited with plenty of surrounding space, while at the other end there is a swing.

### THE TERRACE

The terrace is the main eating and entertaining area of the garden and is a focal point for the adult part of the garden. At its widest, it is 6.5m (19ft), and it is raised 15cm (6in) above ground level so that the edge forms useful extra seating. The brick trim around the edge of the terrace provides an effective visual link with the brick of the house.

### THE LAWN

The lawn is subject to heavy use so, to keep it looking presentable, it has been edged with a brick trim, which also helps to define and accentuate the strong curves of its shape.

The dense evergreen hedge that frames part of the lawn forms a suitable, thick green 'net' for lobbing tennis balls back and forth over, and is sturdy enough not to suffer in the process. Ball games are encouraged in the dormant season only.

### A WOODLAND BOUNDARY

At the far end of the garden, there is a narrow 3m (9ft) strip devoted to woodland. This small, wild area is also home to a garden shed, compost heap, rabbit hutch and sand pit. The pathway, with its surrounding tough planting, is used for chase and hide-and-seek.

**THE PLAN**
1. Bubble fountain
2. Sand pit
3. Woodland edge
4. Play area
5. Terrace
6. Dense evergreen hedge
7. Climbing frame
8. Swing/pergola
9. Pets' corner
10. Tough plant border

*This swing is sited at the end of a series of three archways which form a staggered pergola, highlighting a diagonal axis across the garden and providing a link between the two areas. The structure is both light in appearance and helpful to twining climbers, such as honeysuckle, encouraging them to clothe the frame quickly to provide a sweetly scented play structure.*

A bubble fountain is a simple, safe and attractive water feature for a family garden. Sited next to the terrace and surrounded by pebbles and bold planting, it can be readily viewed from the house. The fountain attracts a variety of birds, which come to bathe in it, and these too are enjoyable to observe.

From the raised terrace, the first archway frames the view out to the garden, leading the eye along the pathway to the swing at the end. The first part of the path is built from the same brick and flagstone used in the terrace but later becomes stepping stones set in grass as the garden becomes more natural.

# A Small City Garden

THIS SMALL GARDEN (13.5M/44FT AT ITS LONGEST) WAS DESIGNED FOR A COUPLE WITH TWO YOUNG DAUGHTERS. THEY WANTED A GARDEN THAT THEY COULD USE FOR ENTERTAINING BUT THAT WOULD ALSO PROVIDE PLENTY TO INTEREST THE WHOLE FAMILY. AS IT IS HIGHLY VISIBLE FROM THE HOUSE, THE VIEWS NEED TO BE INTERESTING THROUGHOUT THE YEAR.

A raised terrace with a bold pattern of brick and paving and wide steps spilling on to the lawn forms the main eating and entertaining area. It includes a built-in sandpit with raised brick walls and, to prevent the neighbours' cats fouling it, a light, flexible and attractive cover made of thin wooden battens, laid close together and attached by two strips of webbing. The numerous pots filling this terrace area can be rearranged seasonally, ensuring that the views from the house are always especially colourful near the building.

The main focal point of the garden is the small building which sits over the informal pool. Wide timber stepping stones lead across and up to another, narrower, paved area which is raised above the water. There is an underwater safety grid just below the surface of the pool. The maximum depth is 600mm (2ft) which does not pose a safety threat now the children are competent swimmers, so the guard will probably be removed in the near future. Aquatic and marginal plants grow in the water, and dragonflies, newts, frogs and birds provide interest.

## THE STRUCTURE

A climber-clad wooden pergola leads around the end of the pool and up to the raised terrace. Under the pergola, a canvas playhouse has been made by using the wooden beam of the pergola as the ridge support and driving two long wooden pegs into the wall to form side supports. The walls and roof are of heavy canvas, with a door and windows cut out. The canvas cover is removed in the winter, but in summer the playhouse is popular with the children and is also used as a bird hide as it allows a good view of the water.

The swing seat, made in canvas to match the playhouse, provides another focal point and is a comfortable spot from which to observe most of the garden.

## THE PLANTING

Apart from on the terrace and the area around the water, the planting is predominantly composed of blue or white flowering species and some purple foliage plants. Tough plants are positioned on the border edges: several hebes, including the glaucous-leaved *Hebe albicans*, *Nepeta faassenii* (catmint), blue-foliaged *Eucalyptus gunnii* (kept as a tough and attractive shrub by annual coppicing), blue buddleias, swathes of *Ajuga reptans* 'Atropurpurea' and *Anthemis cupaniana*, with its profusion of daisy-like flowers. In the summer several large pots of brilliant blue *Agapanthus* are placed in any available gaps in the borders, heightening the effect of the blue-and-white colour scheme, which ties the garden together in a bold but simple fashion.

*ABOVE This is the main eating area next to the house, and even in a small garden it is well worth making it a generous-sized space as here. The planting, patterns of granite setts, containers and furniture all contribute to beautifying the space and reducing the dominance of the main paving material.*

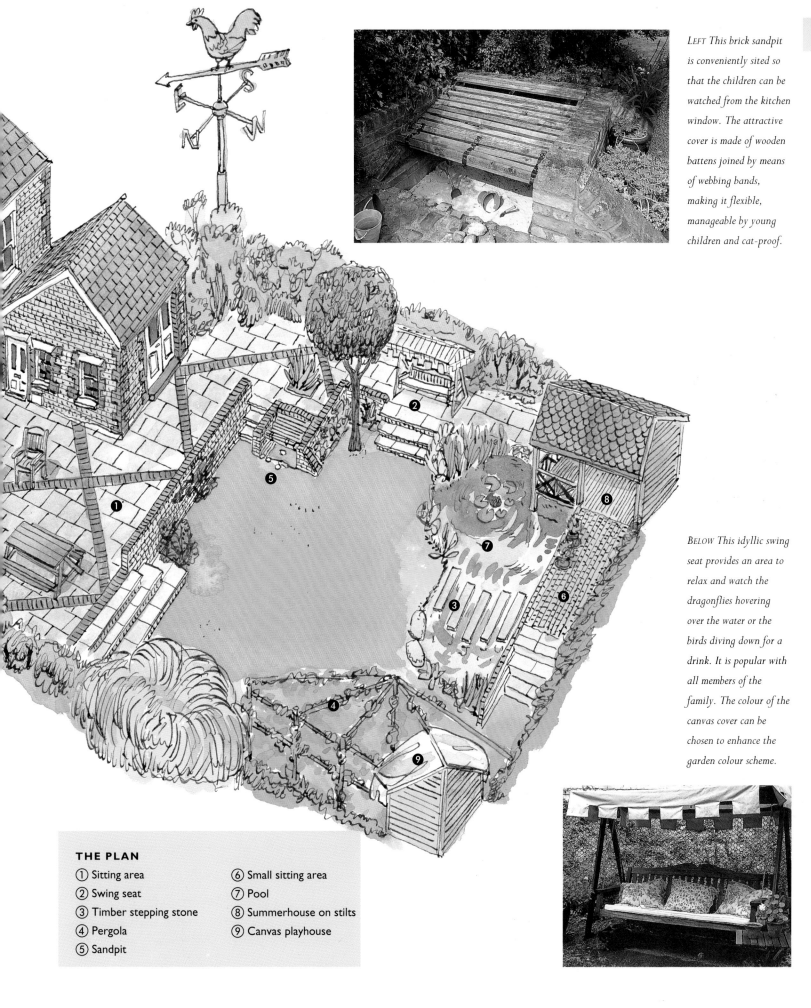

*LEFT This brick sandpit is conveniently sited so that the children can be watched from the kitchen window. The attractive cover is made of wooden battens joined by means of webbing bands, making it flexible, manageable by young children and cat-proof.*

*BELOW This idyllic swing seat provides an area to relax and watch the dragonflies hovering over the water or the birds diving down for a drink. It is popular with all members of the family. The colour of the canvas cover can be chosen to enhance the garden colour scheme.*

**THE PLAN**

① Sitting area
② Swing seat
③ Timber stepping stone
④ Pergola
⑤ Sandpit
⑥ Small sitting area
⑦ Pool
⑧ Summerhouse on stilts
⑨ Canvas playhouse

# A Farmhouse Garden

EACH PART OF THIS HALF ACRE PLOT, WHICH IS MAINTAINED BY ITS OWNER IN JUST A FEW HOURS PER WEEK, HAS A DISTINCT CHARACTER AND FUNCTION. THE GARDEN'S KEY ELEMENTS OF VARIETY AND PRACTICALITY MAY BE BUILT INTO GARDENS OF ALL SIZES.

When visitors arrive, they enter a farmyard flanked by stone barns on two sides. This area has been treated simply with expanses of grass, trees and gravel to retain the farmyard feel. The section of yard in front of the house has been partially separated from the rest by a line of stone pillars linked by wooden beams. This semi-enclosed area has been designed and planted to create a more formal courtyard garden, which is attractive all the year round and provides a sheltered sitting area.

## THE POTAGER
From the courtyard, a passage through the building leads to the small potager, or ornamental kitchen garden. It is divided by paths into six rectangular beds, parts of which are framed by low box hedges and contain topiary and standard gooseberry bushes as well as herbs (*see pages 96–9*).

## THE PLAY LAWN
Walking from the potager to the orchard, you pass through the rough games area. Rides on the ivy-clad rustic double swing (*see pages 62–3*) give exhilarating views over the countryside. A yew hedge divides this cultivated area from the orchard.

## THE ORCHARD
Mown or trodden paths lead through the long grass and wild flowers while mature, strong-limbed fruit trees provide for climbing and support a commando net, trapeze bar, monkey swing and twizzler. The orchard is also used for all kinds of imaginative play: stalking, den-making, jungle adventures and picnics. At the edge, behind a native hedge of *Crataegus monogyna* (hawthorn), *Rosa canina* (dog rose), *Viburnum opulus* (guelder rose) and *Ligustrum vulgare* (wild privet), are the animal houses, cold frames and nursery plot.

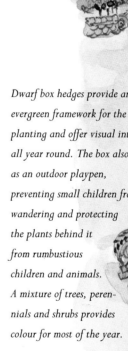

*Dwarf box hedges provide an evergreen framework for the planting and offer visual interest all year round. The box also acts as an outdoor playpen, preventing small children from wandering and protecting the plants behind it from rumbustious children and animals. A mixture of trees, perennials and shrubs provides colour for most of the year.*

## THE WALLED GARDEN
Narrow double gates lead from the orchard to the walled garden at the back of the house with a wildlife pool at its centre. Double rows of pleached hornbeams flank the long sides of the pool and at the end of one is the playhouse.

**THE PLAN**
1. Courtyard
2. Productive family potager
3. Double swing and rough games area
4. Orchard with sandpit
5. Cold frames and animal runs
6. Wildlife pool
7. Playhouse
8. Terrace and barbecue
9. Parking and outhouses

The cow parsley surrounding this sturdy apple tree creates a screen around a very popular spot for play. The different features attached to the tree can be moved up to higher limbs as the children's agility develops so that they maintain interest.

This swing, sited on the games lawn, allows expansive views over the ha-ha, or boundary ditch, to the rolling countryside beyond. The line of telegraph poles which previously marred this view were reused in the construction of the ha-ha.

# A Country Garden

A LOW-MAINTENANCE, HIGH INTEREST GARDEN SUITABLE FOR A FAMILY WITH OLDER CHILDREN AND TEENAGERS.
THE LARGE GARDEN AREA ALLOWS ROOM FOR A NUMBER OF MAJOR FEATURES INCLUDING AN EXTENSIVE
TERRACE, LARGE POOL AND HERB AND VEGETABLE GARDENS.

When I was asked to re-design this garden, it not only required too much maintenance, but also failed to provide sufficient interest. The family, which included two
young children, required an easier-to-manage garden that gave them more pleasure.

### THE FRONT GARDEN

Visitors approach the house from a drive, flanked on one side by a high coniferous hedge which,
prior to redesign, dominated the whole front garden. By reducing the height of the coniferous
hedge by a third and planting a line of deciduous trees in front of it, the oppressive impact of the
massive green hedge was dispelled. The planting is kept to small, formal, box-edged beds filled
with English roses, topiary and trouble-free herbaceous plants.

### THE TERRACE

At the back of the house, a paved terrace is used for barbecues, entertaining and relaxation. I
widened the paved area to 5m (15ft) and extended it along the whole length of the house to
allow space for larger parties and to free the house which previously appeared cramped and
hemmed in. As the house is tucked into a slope, it worked best to divide the terrace into four
different levels, each separated by steps which provide extra seating.

### ADDING A WATER FEATURE

The circular pool, partially surrounded by a bog garden, provides much
interest. Because the house sits in a dip with the garden sloping towards
it, the pool is situated almost 1m (3ft) higher than the terrace making it
a prominent feature when viewed from the house and terrace.

### THE ORCHARD AND PERGOLA

At the south side of the lawn, an archway cut through the high hedge
leads to a new orchard. Here, a mown path leads through longer grass
and wild flowers to a tree house, where the children have their own
hideaway. This wild area is largely the children's domain and is separated from the vegetable garden by a climbing pergola (*see page 64*).

### THE VEGETABLE GARDEN

As the vegetable garden can be seen from the terrace, there is an em-
phasis on the attractive perennial crops, such as globe artichokes,
rhubarb and seakale. It has a sunny site near to the kitchen and is
divided into four small, easy-to-work beds.

*The paved terrace runs
the length of the house
but is divided into four
areas, separated by
generous steps. French
windows have been
added to the house to
make access to the
terrace more convenient.*

**THE PLAN**

| | |
|---|---|
| ① Low conifer hedge | ⑥ Archway |
| ② Herb garden | ⑦ Play pergola |
| ③ Terrace | ⑧ Vegetable garden |
| ④ Circular pool | ⑨ Tree house |
| ⑤ Bog garden | ⑩ Football goal posts |

In front of the house, box-edged beds are arranged in a simple pattern and surrounded by gravel; the small herb garden is ideally situated by the kitchen door. The containers, box hedging and paving slabs give this area year-round interest.

Wide stone steps lead up from the terrace to this large, circular pool which is 7m (20ft) in diameter. Water plants are grown in baskets, instead of being planted directly in a layer of soil spread over the base of the pool, giving more control over planting. Pebbles laid at a gentle slope on one side of the pool allow easy access for small mammals and amphibians.

# The Wind in the Willows Garden

THE MAGICAL WATERSIDE LANDSCAPE EVOKED BY KENNETH GRAHAME IN *THE WIND IN THE WILLOWS* PROVIDED

THE INSPIRATION FOR THIS ENCHANTING GARDEN WITH RIVER, BEACH AND WATERSIDE PLANTING.

To illustrate that children's and adults' demands on a garden are not totally incompatible, for the 1994 Chelsea Flower Show I designed a theme garden based on Kenneth Grahame's well-loved children's story, *The Wind in the Willows*.

Inspired by my own children's enthusiasm for water I felt confident that water features could be safely incorporated into what was primarily a children's garden. The river divides into three parts each representing a different water environment.

### THE RIVER

The first part of the river forms a deep pool (60–90cm/24–36in) in front of Ratty's house, and has an underwater metal safety grid made out of reinforcing mesh, painted black, and positioned 5cm (2in) below the water surface (*see page 112*). To conceal the mesh, water lilies and irises were planted to grow through it. The next section of river is just 5cm (2in) deep; sparkling water races over coloured pebbles and gravel, with many marginal plants adding further interest. The final section, separated by another weir, is a drainable paddling pool made to look like part of the river, with flat pebbles set in concrete forming the base. Around this, a beach of sand and pebbles makes a sizeable 'sand pit'.

Ratty's house creates a focal point at the top of the river. Set into a bank, its chimney can be climbed in order to reach the meadow turf roof, spangled with wild flowers. On one side a large, hollow willow tree forms a den and a play boat is moored to the decking by the front door. Four tiny beds planted with bedding plants and vegetables make up Ratty's garden.

### THE RIVER-BANK PLANTING

Along the river-bank, ferns and ivies tolerate the ravages wrought by children and create an informal riverside feel. The long grass is punctuated by daisies, ragged robins and cowslips. These were planted in the form of small plugs, a successful way to establish wild flowers in the garden.

The boundary between the children's plot and the paddling pool is the main area for ornamental planting. To keep the garden fairly natural in appearance and to make the most of easy-to-grow plants, the planting is limited to vigorous types such as *Centranthus ruber*, *Polygonum bistorta* 'Superbum', *Polgonatum multiflorum*, *Hesperis matronalis*, and *Geranium phaeum*. The evergreen element is mainly made up of *Ajuga reptans* 'Atropurpurea'.

*A climbing tree, made from a dead apple tree set in concrete, has pieces of dowelling fixed into the trunk to form steps and a swing with plaited rope hung from a sole remaining branch (see page 67).*

### THE PLAN

1. Deep pool with under-water grid
2. Shallow, running water
3. Drainable paddling pool
4. Ratty's house
5. Chimney through which children may climb
6. Hollow willow treehouse
7. Ratty's garden
8. Sand pit with swivel log cover
9. Dead climbing tree and swing
10. Beach with sand and pebbles
11. Hammock

The idyllic riverside residence that is Ratty's house was made for exhibition use only. To re-create the house as a permanent feature, a blockwork construction with a reinforced concrete roof would be necessary, as it is damp and bears a heavy load.

Informal planting maintains the riverbank feel and is taken right up to the edge of the paddling pool. The base of the paddling pool is made of flattish pebbles set into concrete, and the sand and pebble beach beside it forms an exciting area for play.

# PLAYHOUSES
# AND
# TREE HOUSES

*A playhouse or tree house provides a wonderful base for*

*recreation for children and adults, offering a private*

*refuge quite separate from the house. Honeypots such*

*as these are ideal for younger children, who will tend*

*to focus their activities around them, easing the*

*pressure on other parts of the garden. An added bonus*

*is that they can be a visual delight as well.*

# The Magic of Playhouses

In today's theme-led world, manufactured playhouses may range from pirate ships to fairy-tale castles, but the more traditional designs owe much to the original 'Wendy house' as featured in the stage production of J.M. Barrie's children's story *Peter Pan* published in 1904. In the story, Peter asks Wendy what her dream house would be and she describes a tiny woodland house 'with funny red walls and a roof of mossy green'. Peter and the Lost Boys rapidly construct a playhouse to this design and Wendy's dream comes true. Few early Wendy houses survive today, although there is an enchanting one at Castle Drogo in Devon, England; named Baby Bunty, it dates from the 1930s just after the castle was complete.

*When Peter Pan and the lost boys constructed the original Wendy House to Wendy's precise specifications, they did so quite spontaneously using readily available materials (the chimney was made from a hat and the door knocker was a shoe). All Wendy Houses benefit from these individual touches.*

### A ROYAL FAVOURITE

For generations, children of the British royal family enjoyed playhouses which were really fully equipped miniature houses. After the formality of the royal nursery, it must have seemed a dream come true for the children to have a child-size place of their own, where they could rule the roost and come and go as they pleased. Queen Victoria and Prince Albert's home at Osborne on the Isle of Wight once had a miniature fortress built by Prince Arthur when he was a boy. The fortress was eventually replaced by the chalet-style Swiss Cottage, which is two storeys high and boasts a tiled and fully equipped kitchen. But for complete sophistication. Queen Elizabeth II's miniature thatched cottage, given to her on her sixth birthday, is hard to better. The house not only has a bedroom, bathroom, sitting room and kitchen but also electricity, gas, hot and cold running water and sheets and blankets embroidered with the royal crest.

### A WORLD OF MAKE-BELIEVE

Fortunately most children are pleased with much simpler structures. Indeed, very small children will derive great pleasure from a blanket thrown over a table or even a large cardboard box with a hole for the door. Much of the delight of a playhouse focuses around mimicking adult activities and if the playhouse is quite simple it will be a springboard for a whole range of imaginative games. With the bare minimum of props it will be a hide-out for outlaws one day and a fire station the next.

*This picturesque gypsy caravan in the late Roald Dahl's garden provides an alternative form of playhouse or garden building. Large enough to live in, it could double as guest accommodation when numbers swell.*

From the child development point of view, playhouses are valuable in that they encourage children to develop communication skills and allow shy or introverted children to play alongside other children in a relaxed adult-free environment. Above all, a playhouse is a place to which a child can escape when the stresses and strains of the adult house become too much. Useable throughout the year, it is an especially valuable outdoor play structure becoming particularly magical in wet weather when the rain beats down on the roof.

### SITING A PLAYHOUSE

Careful siting of a playhouse is important if one is to retain the character of the garden and provide the children with ample opportunity to play with some degree of privacy. As soon as the children are old enough to play for short periods without being in constant view of an adult, it is best for all the family if the house is tucked away in a quiet corner. As most houses are fairly bold in design, they are best sited in a leafy glade or near large shrubs. The foliage will both add to the fairy-tale atmosphere and diminish the presence of the structure for the gardeners in the family. If you have the space, add on a small garden for vegetables, flowers and favourite plants (*see pages 154–7*). A low fence, gate or archway will provide a structure for climbers and further define the children's territory.

### CHOOSING A DESIGN

The first important decision is whether to purchase a manufactured playhouse or make one yourself. Off-the-shelf playhouses come in an enormous range of styles and sizes from

*The heart-shaped detailing on the shuttered window, gives this small playhouse great appeal to children. Large pots with specimen plants in them help anchor the building into its space, and the white wall provides a good backdrop for them.*

*ABOVE This is a ready-made elevated playhouse constructed from oak, with a pitched oak shingle roof complete with a balcony. Sited adjacent to some trees, it will take on the feel of a tree house but it is attractive enough to stand alone like a little house on stilts.*
*LEFT A manufactured playhouse has been given personal touches with the addition of window boxes and planting. This particular one was obtained second-hand, giving it a weathered appearance which helps it blend with the rest of the garden.*

wooden structures in elaborate Georgian style with many rooms through to simple plastic boxes. The play value of smaller ones is fairly limited so if you are looking at this end of the scale a tepee made out of beech branches (*see page 42*) may prove just as rewarding at a fraction of the price. The entertainment value to be derived from larger off-the-peg models, however, particularly ones which incorporate some form of climbing structure, may sustain your children through to their early teens.

If you decide to make your own playhouse there is greater scope for creating a style that suits the mood of your garden and it need not entail elaborate woodwork: a few rustic poles clad with dense trellis and gaps cut for windows would provide a much loved place for

*RIGHT This playhouse, bought in kit form, was erected at the bottom of the garden with a tiny vegetable garden on one side and a flower garden on the other. The area is contained with a home-made hazel fence.*

adventure and so would a willow house (*see page 40*). Playhouses which are partially underground have great appeal as the semi-darkness makes them exciting yet very secure. They are, however, quite complex to build usually requiring a reinforced concrete roof to hold up the turf or planting on top. A space-saving idea is to divide a playhouse in half with a partitioning wall to provide garden storage on one side and a play area on the other. Construct a child-scale door to access the play area and a larger door for the storage side to enable you to manipulate garden machinery reasonably easily.

*This fine playhouse, tucked into a corner of a city garden, forms an exciting yet safe play area for young children. It has been designed to complement the garden, with the two-storey building maximizing the space for use while at the same time providing an excellent lookout post. The planting links the structure to the garden.*

## A SAFE HAVEN

Provided the house is constructed strictly according to instructions and that you buy off-the-shelf playhouses from accredited manufacturers, there are few dangers from this sort of play structure provided it is used for the purpose for which it was designed. I once witnessed a particularly boisterous group of boys sitting on our Wendy house roof holding a toddler's car (complete with one small boy inside) prior to launching it towards the ground. Even the safest items of play equipment require a level of adult supervision appropriate to the age of the users. A hinged door may also be a hazard for young children with fingers getting trapped and some members of the group getting stuck either inside or out. The solution is to leave the house without a door or else to supervise play.

# PROJECT: A WENDY HOUSE

This is a flexible design which can be adapted according to taste. The shutters may be cut into a different shape; the external paintwork can be changed or abandoned in favour of wood stains; and a number of extra features may be added including a house name-plate, shelves, hooks, furniture, window boxes and a small fenced garden.

## GETTING STARTED

Start with the floor and lay some inexpensive paving, a little larger than the floor area of the house – approximately 2.2 x 2.5m (86 x 98in) – on which the house can sit. It is important that water does not collect around the base of the plywood as this will rot the timber, so make sure that the paving is either laid to a fall of about 1:40, taking the water away from the walls, or else lay it with wide 20mm (¾in) joints filled with free-draining gravel.

When you order the six sheets of plywood

### YOU WILL NEED
• Paving slabs: eight for the base, 600 x 600mm (24 x 24in); four slabs 900 x 600mm (36 x 24in); and aggregate, sand and mortar with which to lay them
• Six sheets of 19mm (¾in) thick, exterior grade plywood (WBP),1220 x 2440mm (48 x 96in), cut to the sizes stated in the instructions
• Four wooden battens, 38 x 38 x 1140mm (1½ x 1½ x 44¾in)
• Two wooden battens, 38 x 38 x 2240mm (1½ x 1½ x 88¼in)
• One wooden ridge beam, 19 x 75 x 2440mm (¾ x 3 x 96in)
• Two wooden strips, 19 x 75 x1625mm (¾ x 3 x 96in)
• Two wooden strips, 19 x 75 x 490mm (¾ x 3 x 19¼in)
• Two wooden strips, 19 x 100 x 2440mm (¾ x 4 x 96in) All timber (excluding plywood) to be planed all round (PAR), tanalized softwood

• Wire nails, 32mm (1¼in) long
• Screws, No. 8, countersunk 32mm (1¼in) long
• Screws, No. 8, countersunk 38mm (1½in) long
• Weatherproof wood glue
• Two 305mm (12in) T-hinges for door, black japanned
• Door knob
• Magnetic door closer
• Fourteen 102mm (4in) T-hinges for shutters, black japanned (for front and one end panel)
• Eleven gate hooks and eyes with screw ends as shutter catches, galvanized
• Primer, undercoat and gloss paint

### Tools
• Power jigsaw • Tenon saw • Drill, power or hand
• Drill bits for No. 8 screws • Countersinker
• Screwdriver, power or hand • Hammer

required for the Wendy house, ask the timber merchant to cut the front and back panels for you – they are both 2360 x 1220mm (93 x 48in). Also get the two sides cut to 1825 x 1220mm (71¾ x 48in), reserving the two smaller rectangles left over; from these you

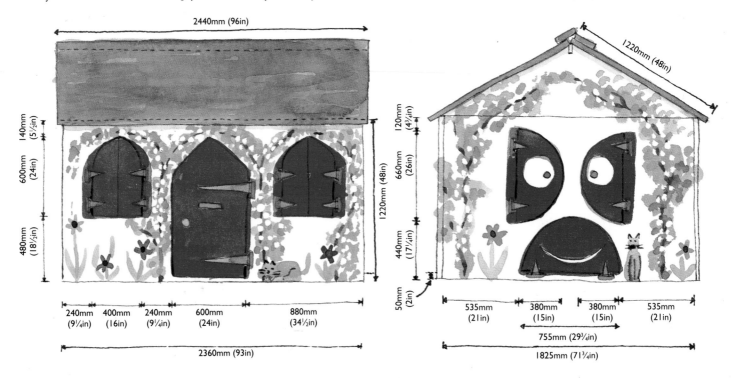

will cut four triangles to add on to the sides. The roof panels are both complete sheets of plywood 1220 x 2440mm (48 x 96in).

### FRONT AND BACK PANELS

Fix the four 38 x 38 x 1140mm (1½ x 1½ x 44¾in) wooden battens to the backs of the front and back panels as shown, parallel to the short end of the sheet and 20mm (¾in) away from it. The bases of the battens are to be 30mm (1¼in) from the bottom and their tops 50mm (2in) from the top. It is easiest to mark the position of the battens on the inside of the panels first. Drill clearance holes for No. 8 woodscrews centrally between the marked lines at 300mm (12in) centres. Countersink the holes on the outside face of the panels so that the screw heads will be recessed and can be filled in later. Drill pilot holes through the clearance holes into the battens. Then coat the battens with glue on one side and clamp them on to the panels before, finally, fixing them with woodscrews.

### DOOR AND SHUTTERS ON FRONT PANEL

Proceed next with the door and shutters on the front panel. In the illustration (*page 36*),

an alternative design has been shown for the shutters on the side. Select the preferred design and make the cardboard template. For the gothic shutters, use a sheet of card the size of the window opening, 400 x 600mm (16 x 24in). Fold this in half vertically and mark out half the outline of the shutter so that, once you have cut it out, the unfolded sheet provides a symmetrical template. Use a straight edge to mark the straight lines and a flexi-curve or similar to provide the arch required. Using the template, draw around the shutter outlines on to one of the two 2360 x 1220mm (94 x 48in) panels, making sure it is in the correct position. Care is needed in sawing out. The easiest way to start is by drilling a hole where the hinge will cover it to hide the irregularity of the outline. With a jigsaw, saw very slowly and carefully along the marked shape. Repeat for the other shutter and door. Put aside the cut-out doors and shutters.

### SIDE PANELS

These are made up from a rectangle 1825 x 1220mm (71¾ x 48in) fixed to an isosceles triangle, which is made up of two triangles joined together. The lengths of the triangle sides are 610m (24in) and 932mm (36⅝in),

*We used gothic shutters for both front and side windows of this Wendy house and they contribute greatly to the character of the place.*

❶ Start by marking the positions of the door and windows on the front panel, and screwing and glueing the four wooden battens onto the backs of the front and back panel, as shown.

❷ The two side panels are made up from a rectangle fixed to an isosceles triangle, which is made up of two triangles cut from the board remaining after the sides have been cut.

❸ Mark a design for the side windows on the panel. Fix the two triangles together with a wooden strip, and fix the then-formed isosceles triangle to the side with an additional strip.

with a right angle as shown (fig 2). To fix the two triangles together, glue and screw them along their shorter sides with a strip of wood 19 x 75 x 490mm (3 x ¾ x 19¼in), set 38mm (1½in) from the longer edges. Then fix the joined triangles on to the side panel with the 19 x 75 x 1625mm (¾ x 3 x 64in) strip of wood again glued and screwed with 30mm (1¼in) screws at about 300mm (12in) centres. Prepare both side panels in this way.

Next cut a 75 x 19mm (3 x ¾in) notch out of the apex of the two side panels to take the ridge beam. Decide on the design of the side shutters and make a template; mark this out on the plywood sheet accordingly and carefully saw out as for the front panel.

### FIXING THE PANELS TOGETHER

Now comes the fun part when the Wendy house starts to take shape. Stand the back panel upright, lean it against something or, better still, ask someone to support it.

Stand up the back panel and one of the side panels (with the gable end attached) and, making sure that bottom edges are flush, drill and screw the edge of the side panel to the 38mm (1½in) batten behind the back panel, using the 38mm (1½in) screws – do not glue. These

two sides will now be self-supporting so it is an easy matter to fix the other end panel in the same manner. The front can now be fixed in a similar fashion.

### THE ROOF

The remaining 19 x 75 x 2440mm (¾ x 3 x 96in) long batten is used as a ridge beam. It is slotted into the apex of the gables and nailed to the edge of the panels with two round-headed nails, 32mm (1¼in) long, at each end.

Fix a 38 x 38 x 2240mm (1½ x 1½ x 88¼in) wooden batten to each full sheet of plywood; position it centrally on the length, parallel to one long edge with the far side of the batten 1059mm (41⅝in) from that edge . This measurement must be accurate so that roof panels butt up tightly. Again use glue and 38mm (1½in) screws at about 300mm (12in) centres. Repeat with the other full sheet.

You will now need a strong person to help you. Lift the first of the roofing panels, resting the batten which has been fixed to its lower underside against the top of the back panel. Lower the roofing panel slowly on to the ridge beam, making sure that it overlaps the gable ends equally on either side before nailing it to the panel edges and the ridge beam. This

process will correct any skewing of the side panels when they were fixed to the front and back panels, although it may be better to loosen the screws while the roofing panel is positioned. Repeat lowering and fixing procedure with the second roofing panel.

In order to protect the gap at the apex of the roof, screw two 19 x 100 x 2440mm (¾ x 4 x 96in) strips of timber over the middle joint, using 32mm (1¼in) screws, with one overlapping the edge of the other.

### FINISHING DOOR AND SHUTTERS

Cut the shutters in half vertically, if using the gothic design. Screw on the hinges and fix the shutters to the house. It may be necessary to chamfer the inside edge of each shutter to facilitate opening and closing. Screw gate hooks and eye catches to shutters and walls so shutters may be held open and closed (three gate hooks and eye catches per pair of shutters). Screw the hinges on to the door, then fix the door on to the house (*see page 35: A safe haven*); fit a door knob and a magnetic closer. If you wish to paint the exterior, prime and undercoat, then gloss the walls, door and shutters with the chosen colour. Alternatively, finish with a wood stain.

❹ Prop up the side panel at right angles to the back panel and screw the edge of the side panel to the batten on the back of the back panel. Repeat with the other side panel.

❺ The long batten or ridge beam is slotted into the two notches which you have cut out of the apexes in the two side panels. This is then nailed firmly into position to the panel edges.

❻ Lift one roof panel into position and nail, then repeat with the second roof panel. Protect the roof gap with the timber strips. Finish cutting the windows and fix the shutters and doors.

# Willow Houses

Willow houses are very satisfying to make as they are simple, inexpensive and fun. Willows are well known for the ease with which most of them root from leafless cuttings or even from stems several years old. The vigorous varieties will even root from lengths as long as 2.4–3.6m (8–12ft). The other helpful factor is their rapid growth rate, which ensures that your willow tunnel, tepee or igloo will, in good conditions, be covered with a curtain of greenery in the first season.

## A NATURAL PLAY STRUCTURE

This design (*below left*) combines a willow tepee with a willow tunnel entrance, a small, informal butyl liner pool with some large boulders and logs, and a recessed area which forms a partially sunken den.

*LEFT This green tunnel of willow is a robust play structure that provides an ideal base for a multitude of games. Encourage children to develop their playground by ringing the changes: add different annual climbers, a willow porch or lookout post.*

*RIGHT This tepee has great scope for development. Long willow shoots form the* uprights, tied together at the top. To gain some instant privacy inside the house, weave cut pliable shoots around the sides. When the living willow shoots grow these can then in turn be woven in.

*ABOVE The addition of a tunnel to a willow tepee greatly enhances its play value. By allocating this sort of play space to your children to shape as they please,* *you will be providing great opportunities for creative play which will often centre around building and 'improving' the space as much as playing in it.*

# PROJECT: A CROCODILE WILLOW HOUSE

The main ingredient needed for this splendid crocodile is a copious supply of long willow cuttings. The varieties of *Salix* best suited to this structure are *Salix triandra* (almond-leafed willow) and *Salix viminalis* (common osier). Several other larger shrub or small tree willows will do, but avoid *Salix caprea* (goat willow), which does not sprout so well, and *Salix fragilis* (crack willow) which, as the name suggests, is brittle and much less pliable than the recommended species.

## METHOD

Between autumn and spring, on clean soil free of perennial weeds, mark out your crocodile on the ground. Then dig a narrow trench, 10cm (4in) wide and 15cm (6in) deep around the outline. Incorporate some free-draining grit into the back-fill if possible.

Take cuttings of the required length, depending on the proportions of your crocodile. These cuttings are best taken immediately below a leaf axil. If you have difficulty finding long cuttings, take two (or even three) cuttings and bind them where they overlap.

Push the cuttings into the trench bottom as securely as possible. Back-fill the trench. Graduate the length of the cuttings to get the desired curvaceous effect making the tummy large enough for your children to fit into. Water the crocodile until established.

Weave the sides *(Fig 3)* and 'plant' small, thicker stub cuttings to make feet. Maintain by weaving in the new growths.

❶ Dig a trench to form the outline of the crocodile and to make it easier to push in and anchor the willow shoots firmly.

❷ Weave cut branches around the sides to form instant 'walls', leaving gaps for eyes and entrance doorways as required.

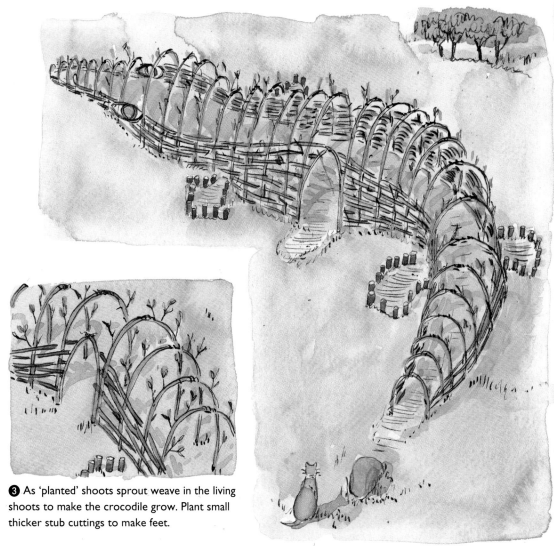

❸ As 'planted' shoots sprout weave in the living shoots to make the crocodile grow. Plant small thicker stub cuttings to make feet.

# Alternative Playhouses

*RIGHT Children appreciate small, personalized spaces which they adapt to suit their current interests. Made from sturdy beech branches bound at the top, this den provides an ideal framework for nasturtiums, sweet peas and runner beans, which everyone can train, cultivate and pick into the bargain. Older children will enjoy the challenge of planning and constructing a den like this as much as they will enjoy using it.*

*BELOW LEFT Dens can be made in so many ways from so many different materials that it makes sense to build them around features which are readily available to you. Making use of a dip in the garden, this den is partially sunken, with a ladder leading down into a well secluded spot. The makeshift frame over the top can be reinforced with climbers, or by weaving in the flexible stems of shrubs, such as elder.*

*ABOVE Even if your children have been brought up in a palace, they will hanker after a tent, but there is no reason why it should not be designed to look striking so that it adds a decorative feature to the garden rather than just cluttering up the lawn. Boldly striped fabrics used to clad a well-proportioned frame make for an excellent tent.*

*BELOW A few manufactured playhouses, such as this one, are multi-functional providing an intriguing range of climbing facilities as well as a home in which children can create a fantasy world. This playhouse is well-made so it does not detract from the garden.*

A hollow tree, should
you have one or find one
that you can move to
your garden, makes a
very special den. This
one is a hollow,
pollarded willow,
converted for children's
use. In A.A. Milne's
Winnie the Pooh stories,
much of the action takes
place in and around
hollow trees which
enhances their natural
charms for children even
further.

# The History of Tree Houses

Tree houses, or 'roosting places' as they were called in Tudor England, are one of the most exhilarating places in which children may play, work and relax. They form a 'nest' perched up high among rustling leaves, giving children a secret vantage point from which to survey the rest of the garden.

Tree houses have long been popular all over the world from Germany, Switzerland and Italy, to South America, Tasmania, India and the South Sea Islands. Today they are regaining their popularity, and deservedly so. Particularly in small gardens in which it can be difficult to accommodate a ground-level building successfully, a tree house may be the answer. By siting the building above eye level, partially camouflaged by branches and leaves, it is much less dominant and blends easily with its surroundings.

### A VARIED HISTORY

Records from the mid-eighteenth century describe Aborigines in Tasmania living in tree houses while in the South Sea Islands, tree house dwellings were widespread – the houses were roughly thatched and access was by means of woven baskets that were raised and lowered as required. In India, Hindu monks and hermits led quiet lives in basic hermitages sited in trees. Today in the Amazonian rain forests, tribes living on flood plains still live on platforms in trees when the rains strike.

Tree houses were also regarded as fashionable garden features. In seventeenth-century Persia, the wealthy created elaborate, shady treetop platforms, decorated with silver and gold and supplied with running water. In the Italian Renaissance, a rather special tree house built in a huge evergreen oak had two stair-

*ABOVE With a little imagination and ingenuity, tree houses can become complete play centres with neighbouring dens for friends and siblings, lookout posts and a number of means of access to fully exploit climbing activities.*

*LEFT Built at Le Mans, France, in the early 1900s, this tree house, and others like it, were called 'Les Robinsons' inspired by Johann Rudolph Wyss's Swiss Family Robinson. Situated in public parks, they were much favoured for picnics. Baskets were lowered on ropes to be replenished with delicacies.*

cases spiralling up to the 8m- (26ft-) wide platform, which contained a marble table, benches and fountains. Later, when romantic, informal gardens were replaced by formal gardens, with elaborate terraces and parterres the tree house went out of favour.

In seventeenth-century England, huge lime trees were pleached (trained and pruned) to create several rooms, at different heights, stacked on top of each other. Wooden planks formed the floors, while the living limbs were trained to provide the enclosures. One well known example at Cobham Hall was three storeys high and constructed in a lime tree, which was pleached to form the chambers. It served as a romantic tree-top banqueting house for more adventurous diners.

## PLANNING PERMISSION

You will certainly need to check the local planning legislation before creating a three storey-high banqueting hall with a pitched roof in your back garden! Furthermore, if the tree in question is protected by a preservation order, or if you live in a conservation area, then it is likely that you will need the approval of your local planning authority. Otherwise much depends on the structure of the tree house and the interpretation of the planning legislation. If the structure is only a few planks lashed to a tree and is meant to be temporary, a planning authority is unlikely to want to get involved. In the UK, however, if the cubic capacity is greater than 10 cubic metres (30 cubic feet), if it is higher than 4m (12ft) [or

*This fantastic building is still standing and has just been renovated. It is in a lime tree at Pitchford Hall in Shropshire and is thought to have been constructed in the early 1700s. Princess Victoria played in it in 1832 when she was thirteen and staying at the Hall.*

3m (9ft) if it has a flat roof] or if it is near a highway or overlooking another dwelling, then it is worth seeking further advice.

## MADE-TO-MEASURE TREE HOUSES

For those who find the prospect of building a tree house too daunting but would like a design that is individual, there are several firms that specialize in making them (*see page 166*). Alternatively your local tree surgeon may be able to put you in touch with a neighbouring firm.

# Choosing a Tree House for Your Family

The essential ingredient of any good tree house is, of course, a suitable tree and its height and structure will to some extent dictate the tree house design. As you will see on the following pages, it is not necessary to have a tree with a wide, branching limb structure. In fact, a tree house can be partially or entirely free-standing. It may be in the tree, by the tree, or even slung between trees.

## SAFETY FIRST

For children between five and ten years old, an old apple tree often provides suitable branches for a tree house. Ideally, the platform should be just 1m (3ft) off the ground and should have a secure balustrade, a minimum height of 750mm (30in), with the gaps between the railings no larger than 100mm (4in). The design of the access is particularly important as this is where most accidents happen, with children fighting, pushing, shoving and racing to get up or down first. To be really safe, make a staircase to the tree house; otherwise position a fixed ladder with bannister at an angle of about 60°. The ladder should have rounded rungs 25–38mm (1–1½in) in diameter, so that children's hands can get a good grip. The treads or rungs should not be too close together or they may trap small feet.

The soil around the base of a tree dries out quickly and can become as hard as concrete. It is a good idea to make a soft landing below the ladder, by providing an area of sand, gravel or bark (*see pages 60–1*).

Young children will need close supervision until their agility is sufficiently developed. If you also have very young children that you want to bar from the treehouse, make the access selective by positioning the first rung

*This tree house is specifically for younger children. The totally enclosed sides make falling out unlikely and there is a small window in one end providing views out. The access points often provide scope for accidents and here a sturdy ladder has been chosen instead of a rope ladder (which would nonetheless be more fun for older children). A hand rail would make the ladder safer still.*

well out of reach, or have a removable ladder.

## ELABORATE OR SIMPLE?

A tree house fulfills a child's need for excitement and fantasy while also providing them with a quiet place of their own. From the aesthetic point of view, they also blend into a garden often adding a magical element which has great charm. If you have the space for it, add extra features to the tree house, such as rope ladders, scramble nets or a trapeze, and it will soon become your children's main focus for play in the garden.

Alternatively, you may want to design a tree house which all the family can enjoy. A rustic design with a pitched roof may be appropriate in some gardens, the roof being either thatched or tiled with wooden shingles. Or for a more sophisticated look, the walls could be made from plywood allowing more elaborately shaped doors and windows in the Gothic or Tudor style, for example. The finish could be rendered or painted with a green or brown stain, or even with Tuscan pink (*see page 55*). If there is the space, a balcony looking out on the garden is a real luxury.

*This high-level tree house in a mature willow provides a vantage point over water meadows. It is built for older children, providing bags of scope for that essential exhilaration factor. The house has been designed to grow with the family, with plans afoot to develop an additional storey.*

# Planning a Tree House

If you are in the enviable position of having a selection of trees in which you could site your tree house, you can afford to be fussy about the one you pick. Ideally, the tree should be healthy, with no signs of rot or decay, no pockets of water collecting in it, and no dead wood in the canopy. Avoid species which tend to shed branches such as horse chestnut and *Robinia pseudoacacia* (false acacia) and for preference choose an oak or an old orchard tree, especially an apple or pear (but not plum).

It is often recommended that the tree should be mature, as building a structure in a rapidly growing young tree may well hinder its natural development. However, if you have an otherwise suitable semi-mature tree in your garden do not necessarily rule it out; just bear in mind that the structure must be able to stand up to the tree's growth without too much dis-

tortion, and the tree must be able to expand without being impeded.

## CHOOSING A TREE

The shape and height of the tree is crucial. A tree with spreading branches will probably not be able to accommodate a platform of useful size without the removal of one or two limbs. If the tree has a preservation order on it or is in a conservation area permission will be required to put a structure in it, and to carry out tree surgery. In a mature oak or lime tree the forking of the branches is likely to be at a significant height, in which case the tree house will be more suitable for teenage children and adults than for small children. In Lincolnshire in England, however, the National Trust have constructed several tree houses over 2m/6½ft from the ground in the play area at Belton

House which, having railings around them and staircase access, are ideal for younger children.

It is not safe to build a house out on a branch, as the weight is entirely supported by a single limb. If this position is the only possible one, rest the structure on the branch and add a framework to make the house self-supporting. As the tree grows, make sure that the supporting network is still secure and is not being pulled out of the ground.

Placing a tree house between two, three or four trunks can be very effective visually. However, when the wind blows the house will move between the supporting trees, which will all flex slightly differently, so the supporting structure must be capable of coping with this. The higher up you place the house the more movement will occur, so do not be too ambitious.

*If you are lucky enough to have a tree with widespread limbs which enable you to build an unsupported tree house, make the most of it.*

*Placing the tree house between two or more trees is a good solution. It is often possible to do this without providing any additional supporting posts.*

*A tree house resting out on a limb is not structurally safe unless you provide it with additional supporting posts as illustrated here.*

*Building the tree house around the trunk is an excellent way to anchor your structure. Additional load-bearing posts will provide much of the support.*

*ABOVE This treehouse is built partially around the tree and is entirely supported on the posts. It has been designed primarily as a dynamic play structure with movable features such as ladders and ropes so that the children can continually develop its play value.*

*ABOVE This tree and tree house provide many movable features to encourage agility as well as offer amusement. As the tree house is mainly above eye level it has less visual impact on the garden than a ground-level climbing frame, for example.*

A self-supporting structure in a tree is often the simplest form of tree house, requiring only minimal damage to the tree. However, if your garden has no suitable trees you can build a house on stilts, with climbers planted to grow up them. Plant three or four young trees (1.2–1.5m/4–5ft high), without stakes, and train the branches around the house. The small planting size will enable them to establish faster, and they can be trained easily. Choose fast-growing trees, for example *Prunus avium* (wild cherry) or a lime such as *Tilia platyphyllos*; both of these grow very large, and are ideal on free-draining limy soils. For a small garden, *Sorbus aucuparia* (mountain ash), which tolerates most soil conditions, would be more suitable. Always remember to check that the force of the growth of the trees is not making the structure unstable.

## CONSTRUCTION

The best method of fixing the structure to the tree is debatable. One arboriculturist of some note has stated that lashing the structure to the tree with man-made rope, as is often recommended, can cause considerable damage, as tree houses are liable to be forgotten about when the children have passed a certain age. This system is acceptable if the ropes are checked regularly throughout the life of the tree, though it is most suitable for mature trees which are not going to grow as rapidly. However, ropes are extremely difficult to loosen as they tighten with the tree growth, so it is believed that the occasional screw fixing into the tree will do less damage.

A heavy-duty pallet makes an ideal platform, but you must shape or pad the edges where it fits in the tree to prevent scarring. If you make your own platform it is better to use softwood rather than hardwood, partly because it is cheaper and lighter but also because if it is forgotten about in years to come it will do less damage to the tree.

When you are planning how to construct the treehouse, aim to make it as light as possible. Exterior-grade ply is ideal for the walls and for the roof, though the latter could be made from treated hardboard or canvas, which would be lighter still. Do not forget that safety is paramount, and the house and tree need to be checked over at least twice a year.

# PROJECT: A CHILDREN'S TREE HOUSE

Few people have in their garden the ideal tree, with spreading boughs, for holding a tree house, so this one is designed to be self-supporting, with all the load on the posts. An old, mature tree can be utilized for additional support, but allow plenty of clearance for growth in younger trees. The height and accessibility of the house may be altered to suit the needs of your family, and the shape of the tree. The platform of this one is 1.8m (6ft) from the ground, and as such only older, agile children should be allowed on it without close supervision. You may possibly need to consult your local planning authority.

Here pallets are used to form a ready-made base. These come in many different sizes, so adaptation may be necessary.

## BUILDING THE PLATFORM

First shape the post tops (*fig 1*). Having decided on the exact position and height of the treehouse, dig four holes 450 x 450mm x 700mm (18 x 18 x 28in) deep in a rectangle, with 1200mm (48in) between the posts on the long sides and 875mm (34½in) between those on the short sides. Put a 50mm (2in) layer of free-draining hardcore or coarse gravel into the base of each hole and ram down. Brace

the posts vertically in the holes, ensuring the tops are correctly positioned to take the roof, and the spacings are correct for the pallets.

Fill the holes with concrete to within 50mm (2in) of the surface. Slope the concrete surface away from the posts to shed water. Check the position of the posts again. When the concrete has set (about 48–72 hours), position the base beams at a height of 1.7m (5ft 8in) (or to suit) across the front and back posts. Fix the beams to the posts with 225mm (9in) coach bolts (*fig 2*).

Lay the pallet on the base beams, front edge midway across the front beam. Drill holes for

## YOU WILL NEED

### House

- One and a half heavy-duty close-boarded matching pallets, 1.2 x 1.2m and 1.2 x 0.6cm (4 x 4ft and 4 x 2ft). Pallets differ, and you may have to vary – but not decrease – timber sizes accordingly.
- Four 3.8m (12ft 6in) hardwood poles for main posts, 125mm (5in) in diameter.
- Two 1.5m (5ft) base beams, 75 x 75mm (3 x 3in).
- Two 1.8m (6ft) crossrails, 75 x 100mm (3 x 4in), planed to fit snugly in pallet.
- Two 2.7m (9ft) diagonal braces 63mm (2½in) in diameter.
- Two 1.2m (4ft) end boards, 125mm x 38mm (5 x 1½in).
- One 3.2m (10ft 6in) ladder side, 75 x 75mm (3 x 3in), free of knots [see note].
- One 2.3m (7ft 6in) ladder side, 75 x 75mm (3 x 3in), free of knots.
- One 870mm (34in) corner post, 85mm (3¼in) in diameter [see note].
- 5.9m (19ft 4in) length of balustrade, 63mm (2½in) in diameter.
- Thirty four 870mm (34in) spindles, 35mm (1⅜in) in diameter [see note].
- Two 1150mm (45in) battens, 50 x 50mm (2 x 2in).
- Nine 1200mm (48in) spindle braces, 75mm (3in) in diameter [see note].

- Seven 600mm (24in) ladder rungs 35 x 50mm (1⅜ x 2in), free of knots.
- Two triangular spacers, approx. 100 x 100 x 70 x 75mm thick (4 x 4 x 2¾ x 3in thick), cut to suit.
- Hardcore or coarse gravel 0.05m³ (0.07cu.yd.).
- Concrete mix 1:6 (cement:ballast), 0.5m³ (0.7cu.yd.).
- Four 225mm (9in) coach bolts with protective coating, M10 (⅜in), plus single coil and flat washers, and nuts.
- Sixteen 200mm (8in) coach bolts (as above). (Lengths may vary depending on thicknesses of wood in pallet and of poles.)
- Three 125mm (5in) and four 150mm (6in) woodscrews.
- Other common sizes of rustproof screws and nails.

### Roof

- Eight 500mm (20in) corner braces, 63mm (2½in) in diameter.
- Two 1450mm (57in) base beams, 35mm x 63mm (1⅜ x 2½in).
- Two 1120mm (44in) base beams, 35mm x 63mm (1⅜ x 2½in).
- Four 1450mm (57in) rafters, 35mm x 63mm (1⅜ x 2½in).
- One 110mm (4⅜in) centre block, cut from 50 x 75mm (2 x 3in) sawn wood.
- 75mm (3in) dowel, 8mm (⁵⁄₁₆in) in diameter.

- One ball finial, 100mm (4in) in diameter.
- Two 1450mm (57in) baseboards, 200 x 19mm (8 x ¾in).
- Two 1120mm (44in) baseboards, 200 x 19mm (8 x ¾in).
- Twenty-four roof battens (varying lengths), 25 x 35mm (1 x 1½in).
- Four 1050mm (41⅜in) lengths of broom handle.
- Wood offcuts or shingles, approx. 150 x 300 x 7mm (6 x 12 x ¼in).
- Rustproof screws and nails.
- Waterproof woodworking adhesive.
- Non-toxic wood preservative.
- **Note:** Hardwood is advisable for the poles. The remaining wood could be hardwood or pressure-impregnated, PAR softwood. Lengths of balustrade timbers and long ladder side are for a 750mm (30in) high balustrade. Adjust accordingly for a 900mm (36in) height.

### Tools

- Portable workbench • Steel measuring tape • Steel rule • Spade • Shovel • Power drill • High-speed wood drill bit • Extension rod • Drill bits • Hammer • Screwdriver • Try square or combination square • Adjustable sliding bevel • Panel saw (or circular saw) • Tenon saw • Dowelling jig • Dowel bit • Wood plane • Spanners • Chisel • Mallet • Hacksaw • File.

coach bolts through each post into the pallet side timbers. Insert the cross rails, one end flush with the back of the pallet, and move the pallet forward so you can continue the holes into the cross rails. Remove the rails and enlarge the holes to fit over the nuts and washers which will secure the pallet to the posts. Reposition the pallet and bolt to the posts.

Replace the cross rails inside the pallet and secure them with one screw through the top of each slat and three screws through each of the pallet side beams. Secure the half pallet in the same way (*fig 3*).

To strengthen the protruding half-pallet (the balcony), run two diagonal braces from the bases of the rear posts against the front posts to the sides of the front pallet; they should finish 85mm (3½in) back from the front edge of the pallet to allow for fixing the corner post and long ladder side. Secure with coach bolts (*fig 4*). The braces will have to bend inwards to the pallet sides. If they will not flex, use a block of wood as a spacer to fill the gap and increase the bolt length.

Fix the end boards over the front and back ends of the platform, with three screws into the end of each of the four pallet rails.

### BUILDING THE ROOF

The roof base beams will lie flat in the recesses cut in the main posts. Assemble them with glue and two screws per joint (*fig 5*). Lie the rectangle flat, pin string lines along the diagonals, then lay the rafters on edge centrally along the string lines; prop them in the centre on an offcut of base beam with a piece of card on top, which will be used to make a template for the roof centre block. Opposing ends of the rafters should be 50mm (2in) apart. Mark across the ends of the rafters on to the card and complete the hexagon so formed (*fig 5*). Cut the block to shape and plane the cut faces. Drill a central hole 25mm (1in) deep for the finial dowel and glue in the dowel. Cut the

❶ Take the four main posts and saw three-quarter segments out of the tops to a depth of 35mm (1⅜in). The four corners of the roof base timbers will sit in these recesses.

❻ Nail the first batten on edge at the bottom of the rafters. Fix the next one flat and parallel to it, 75mm (3in) up the rafters; nail subsequent battens flat and spaced 145mm (5¾in) apart.

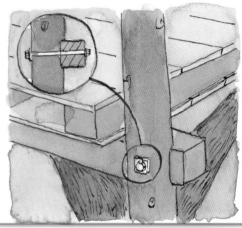

❷ Where the base beams cross the posts, flatten the round posts by removing about 20mm (¾in) with a chisel so the interface is flat on both surfaces.

❼ Lift the completed roof into position on the pre-shaped ends of the main posts so that the roof base timbers rest in the recesses. (This is a job for at least three people.)

bottom ends of the rafters at 32° to the upper face and the top ends at 58°. With help, hold up the rafters against the centre block so it is flush at the bottom. Glue and screw the rafter bottom ends to the base beams, with the ends flush with the corners of the rectangle, and the top ends to the centre block.

Fix battens to the rafters on one surface of the roof at a time (*fig 6*), and cut the ends at an angle along the centre line of the rafters. Screw the baseboards to the bottom two battens, overhanging at the bottom by 50mm (2in); angle the ends as for the battens. Nail

wood offcuts or shingles to the battens, working from the bottom upwards, so that the vertical joints are staggered 75mm (3in) in adjacent rows and each row overlaps the one below by about half its length. Cut the shingles along the line of the rafters at the ends of rows. Nail the top triangular pieces to the projecting centre block. Screw lengths of broom handle to the rafters, then fit the finial.

Fit the roof (*fig 7*) then drill two holes up at an angle in each post; screw through these into the base beams. Screw the corner braces to the base beams and posts (*fig 8*).

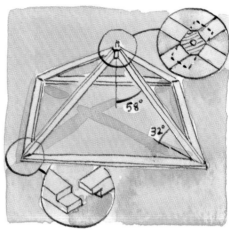

**3** Position the half-pallet over the protruding cross rails and screw it in position to the rails, with one screw through each plank and three screws through each side.

**4** Where the diagonal braces meet the posts and pallet, flatten the rounded surfaces by about 20mm (¾in). Fix them to the posts and pallet sides with 200mm (8in) coach bolts.

**5** Cut a halving (lap) joint at each end of the roof base timbers to join them together. Use the template to mark the end of the 50 x 75mm (2 x 3in) centre block to connect the rafters.

**8** Notch the long ladder side over the pallet with a bird's-mouth joint then cut a triangular spacer to fill the gap. Screw through the ladder side and spacer into the pallet.

**9** Screw the V-shaped braces, angled at the ends, to the underside of the balustrade and to the base or battens. Fit an extra brace from the top of the corner post on the long side.

**10** Place the shorter ladder side firmly in position, parallel to the long ladder side, and secure it to the pallet over a triangular spacer. Cut it flush with the top of the pallet.

### ERECTING THE BALUSTRADE AND LADDER

Flatten the corner post at one end and fix it to the front left side of the pallet with three 125mm (5in) screws. Screw the long ladder side to the front right side (*fig 8*).

Run the balustrade outside the posts, with a gap for access. It should be at least 750mm (30in) high (900mm/36in for larger children). Notch the main posts 20mm (¾in) deep where it crosses them and mitre the balustrade corners. Bolt to the main posts, corner post and long ladder side with 200mm (8in) coach bolts

and skew nail the corners together.

Screw spindles to the inside of the balustrade and the sides of the base, at a maximum of 100mm (4in) apart. At front and back, where the base projects beyond the balustrade, fix the bottom ends to 50 x 50mm (2 x 2in) battens screwed across the pallets if the spindles don't curve enough to allow fixing to the sides. Add V-braces for extra strength (*fig 9*); their length will depend on their position.

Fit the short ladder side (*fig 10*). Round off the top edge of the rungs and screw to the ladder sides, spaced about 250mm (10in) apart.

**General Tips**
• Cut off protruding bolt ends with a hacksaw and file them flush. Treat all timber with two coats of preservative.
• Plant climbers against the posts, avoiding the concrete. Suitable shade-loving plants would be honeysuckle such as *Lonicera japonica* 'Halliana', and/or ivy such as *Hedera colchica* 'Dentata'. Water frequently, as the roots will be competing with those of the tree.
• Check every six months for signs of rot, damage or loose fixings, and check that the tree remains healthy and safe.

# Tree House Variations

*ABOVE LEFT* The solid walls, with just a small window and roof, make this tree house safe for young children. The fixed ladder makes access fairly easy and a hand rail each side of the ladder would make it safer still. Descending from a tree house is often the most dangerous part of playing in one.

*ABOVE CENTRE* This is a real home in the trees. It was made from a converted dog kennel fixed between two tall pine trees. The balcony, although narrow, adds another dimension and enables children to have high-level picnics outside in the sunshine.

*ABOVE RIGHT* Simple but striking, this lofty structure has a pitched roof design and is built high up in a tree. The tree is on top of a hill so treetop dwellers enjoy commanding views over the garden.

Built as a treetop office, complete with computer and fax machine, this tree house has a 2m- (6ft 6in-) square room inside. A balcony provides a small, enchanting area in which to work outside and leads to a high walkway which provides access in a less precipitous form than the ladder. The Tuscan pink render and verdigris paint finish are new but have been hand-mixed and distressed to give a well established look. For paint finishes, it is well worth a little time, trouble and experimentation to achieve an out-of-the-ordinary colour.

OPPOSITE *This ivy-clad tree house, which sits in an old apple tree, was designed and built by Peter Farrell. It is low level and therefore safe for use by the younger members of the family. However, it also incorporates special features, such as a balancing log linked to a climbing structure at one end, to capture the interest of slightly older children.*

# GARDEN
# GAMES

*With more space, more freedom and the stimulation of
the outdoor environment, the garden offers a more
enticing area for play than the house. There is great
scope for providing a wide range of energetic activities,
from exhilarating cable runways to simple rope swings,
while some action-filled games require no more than a
ball and an expanse of lawn.*

# Play Areas

Most children thoroughly enjoy outdoor play equipment, particularly when it offers the opportunity to play with other children. Although these games are apparently just fun, play is not only a pastime but most important to a child's development. While they are absorbed playing pirates on the climbing frame, children are also learning how to control their bodies and interact with their peers.

For children to make the most of play areas, they should be exciting yet safe. The environment should capture their imagination, stimulate and entice them.

### FIRST CONSIDERATIONS

Deciding which item of play equipment to provide will be influenced by the age range of the child or children, the funds available, the size of the garden and, last but most important, what the children enjoy best. Site the equipment so that you can provide the required level of supervision. Although children do like privacy, even older, agile children need to be supervised to some extent. Very young children need constant adult care, so smaller equipment must be sited accordingly.

### SWINGS

The single most popular item of outdoor play equipment has, for a long time, been the swing. This is an exhilarating play feature for children and appeals to a broad age range. A double swing is, of course, much better than a single one, as children will enjoy the companionship and spend less time squabbling. A swing structure can be relatively simple to make (*see page 62*) and, by changing the seats from cradle seats to flat seats, you can adapt it easily for continued use as the children grow.

The height of the frame determines the height of the swing and thereby the degree of exhilaration for children. If you choose a high frame from the start, more monitoring will be necessary when the children are younger.

The swing's harmless appearance and its very familiarity belie the fact that it is also the source of many accidents. Most are caused by the swing (with or without child in place) striking a passer-by with potentially serious results. UK safety regulations require that a single, large swing in a public play area must have a space of about 9 x 4.5m (27 x 13½ft) which is completely free of all other items. To adopt that standard in your garden might preclude a swing altogether, although you may take the view that a public park filled with large numbers of children of all ages is quite different to a private family garden in which numbers rarely exceed ten.

*This 'flying fox' forms a cable runway across the garden allowing children to 'fly' on the pulley from the treehouse across to the other side — it's great fun for adults too! It was designed by Roger Storr.*

Wooden seats on swings, although commonly used, rarely have impact-absorbing edges, and the impact of the seat on a head can be lethal. For this reason it is worth purchasing a flat rubber safety seat, available from specialist manufacturers (*see page 166*). Plastic seats are dangerous as they can splinter on impact causing serious injuries, and old tyres are also not recommended as they contain steel reinforcing wires, which can over time become exposed.

With safety considerations borne in mind the swing is definitely a worthwhile feature, providing wonderful play value for babyhood through to early teens.

## CLIMBING FRAMES

Ready-made climbing frames are not always the easiest items to blend into the garden. Bear in mind that, whereas bright colours go down well in public places, in the garden environment softer, natural colours can be more suitable. Aluminium climbing frames are harsh visually and equally exciting equivalents can be found made of wood, for similar prices.

Building a climbing frame to your own design requires careful thought. It must be stable and capable of taking occasional, larger loads – such as when, after a birthday party, twenty over-fed children cram themselves on to it. In addition, the design must avoid finger traps and head traps, the timber should be planed rather than sawn to avoid splinters, and pressure-treated with preservative for a longer life. The structure should also be bolted and screwed, rather than nailed together. Ensure that the height and scale of the frame is appropriate to the age of the children. It may be necessary to bar younger ones or accept that the older ones will soon tire of it.

Any structure, whether home-made or not, must be thoroughly checked a minimum of three times a year for signs of rotting timbers, frayed ropes, movement of joints and so on, and any problems dealt with accordingly.

The climbing pergola (*see pages 64–5*) has the advantage of toning sympathetically with the garden and another option for a home-made climbing frame is to site it around a tree, especially if it is a good climbing tree. The frame will tend to blend in better with the garden and, when the children start to outgrow the climbing frame, they can then extend their games into the tree, possibly with a linked ladder access. The heights they climb may then become quite considerable, so make sure that they are competent enough to deal with them and supervise them as necessary. Always provide a safe landing surface of bark, sand or gravel (*see page 60*).

Simple climbing structures can be made from logs in various shapes and sizes (*see page 66*), carved to resemble dragons, horses, carts or boats. These can look extremely attractive, are fairly simple to make and appeal greatly to younger children. Simple wooden balancing bars, a series of log stepping stones and horizontal bars of different heights are also easy to make and entertaining.

## CABLE RUNWAYS

A cable runway or flying fox comprises a rope suspended from two points, usually with one end a little higher than the other. A pulley, or travelling crab, runs along the rope with a simple button seat hanging from it. This play feature is suitable for supervised children from about six years old onwards, and even adults find the sensation of whizzing between the two fixed points at speed exhilarating. The fixed points may be the branches of a tree, or a pole fixed to a climbing frame, so long as the area which the traveller passes through is totally unobstructed, as a considerable amount of momentum is built up.

## SLIDES

Slides are usually of metal or plastic, and occasionally of wood. If there is a suitable slope, they are relatively easy to accommodate. If not, you will need the freestanding sort which do not blend easily into the average-sized garden.

*This magnificent play fort, complete with drawbridge and small moat, provides fantastic entertainment value and at the same time gives a magical element to the garden. It was designed by the late Sir Frederick Gibberd, architect of Harlow New Town, England, for his children. The present 'logs' are made of concrete as the originals rotted away.*

# Playing Safe

Play areas should be designed to be exciting, but it is not always easy to balance the thrill factor against the need for safety. Having said that, certain types of equipment and design do cause a high proportion of accidents, and if you avoid these you will not have to worry so much when you hear shrieks from your garden.

## ANTICIPATING ACCIDENTS

As previously noted, one of the most dangerous pieces of equipment is the swing. Compared to cable runways and high slides it appears to be a gentle form of play, but children tend to swing higher and higher and when someone crosses their path they are out of control and unable to prevent a collision. Easy ways to reduce the likelihood of this happening are to site the swing well away from popular routes across the garden and not let toddlers run around unchecked when older children are using the swing. And while an old weathered wooden seat might look charming, with small children they should be avoided on

safety grounds. A flat rubber seat of the type mentioned on page 58 is the best choice for a garden swing.

When you are positioning two or more pieces of equipment together bear in mind that younger children become so absorbed in their own activities that they forget they might injure their neighbour. Children are also impulsive – when they decide that they want to play on something they go straight for it, regardless of whether this will take them into the path of moving equipment or hurtling bodies. Make sure that the pieces are positioned so that the likelihood of collisions is minimized.

Accidents often happen at the access point to a piece of equipment, such as the ladder up to a tree house or the top of a slide from a climbing frame. Children will push and shove if someone is delaying, so pay particular attention to these areas. Make sure that handles are available for gripping, that there are no traps for feet or articles of clothing to get caught in, and that ladder rungs are the right shape and size for children's hands to grip firmly.

Children will always push every piece of equipment to the limit. As they become older they will tire of simply going inside a Wendy house and will want to climb on top, walk along the ridge or slide down the roof. Remove the equipment if the children have grown too old for its proper use or point out the dangers. Bear in mind, too, that a group of raucous children will embark upon hazardous play they would think twice about in more sober moments.

Most play equipment in private gardens is designed for small numbers of children. The tolerance and loading foreseen in the original design does not usually allow for the numbers that may be present at birthday parties and family get-togethers, so keep a careful eye on popular areas on such occasions.

Do not forget the need for regular maintenance. The level of supervision needed reduces as children become more agile and able on their favourite pieces of equipment, but they will also be testing it to the full by doing new and different things with it. Each new season

## TYPES OF SAFETY SURFACE

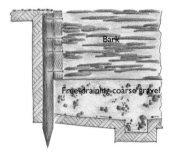

*To construct a safety surface from bark, excavate the area and lay 15cm (6in) granular material for drainage. Lay geotextile membrane over it, then spread 30cm (12in) of bark. The sides here are contained by timber planks nailed to stakes.*

*Here the safety surface is composed of 30cm (12in) of rounded particle gravel, laid on a geotextile membrane on top of 15cm (6in) of drainage material. The gravel is contained by a row of round poles driven into the ground adjacent to one another.*

*Sand 30cm (12in) deep is raised above ground and contained by horizontal logs nailed to vertical stakes. This is necessary for excessively wet conditions.*

*As children outgrow equipment they will use it in new, potentially dangerous ways to increase the thrill.*

*The access point to play equipment is usually the most hazardous, so pay particular attention to design here.*

*Swings are one of the most dangerous pieces of equipment. Site them where people will not run in front.*

*Restrict access during parties unless the design allows for extremely heavy loads, and check the structure first.*

or at least twice a year, check that equipment is in good order.

When you are constructing or mending items the general rule is to avoid using nails as they can pull out more easily than a screw or bolt. Use stainless steel or good-quality zinc-plated fixings. Make sure that any protruding ends of bolts are cut off and filed smooth, and paint the ends with a zinc-rich paint.

### LAYING A SAFETY SURFACE

If you provide a safety surface under equipment you will reduce the severity of any accidents. Grass is quite absorbent if there has been regular rainfall, but in dry periods (often when the garden is most used) and in winter it can become hard and abrasive. Bark, sand and gravel make suitable safety surfaces for private gardens. For aesthetic effect it is best to sink the safety surface so that it is flush with the ground rather than raised above it. However, if you are in an area which does not drain well or has a high water table you will need to raise the surface above ground level or put in drainage, particularly if you are using bark, which will rot down quicker if permanently wet.

**Bark** is increasingly popular as it has excellent impact-absorbing qualities (better than sand or gravel) and is easy to install. Ideally it should be laid to a depth of 30cm (12in), although 20cm (8in) is better than nothing. The best is a granular bark which comes mainly from pine trees (*Pinus* spp.), as opposed to the stringy, elastic bark from spruce (*Picea* spp.). You can buy two grades, one with a particle size of 8–25mm ($5/16$–1in) which is more user-friendly for young children, and the other with a particle size of 10–50mm ($7/16$–2in) for larger children; both have similar shock-absorption characteristics. The bark should have no fine dust, coarse angular fragments or additives.

Having spread the bark, allow it to settle and then top it up. It will become displaced easily and will need raking to maintain an even depth and to loosen it up. Check regularly that no cans or stones have strayed into it.

**Sand** is loved by most children for its soft, fine texture. Its drawback is that cats love it too, so if cats use your garden it is best to avoid sand as it is difficult to protect a large area from cat mess. Alternatively, be strict with hygiene. The type of sand required is critical

– avoid using a sharp building sand, which has interlocking particles and forms a hard, non-shock-absorbing surface; if it forms a good sandcastle, do not use it. The particles must be 0.25–1.5mm (less than $1/16$in across) and rounded, so air spaces remain between them, and should be white or non-staining. The sand should be laid to a depth of 30cm (12in) and will need regular raking.

**Gravel** is rarely used, although in certain sites it will be aesthetically pleasing. The particles must be rounded rather than angular so they do not interlock when compressed but have cushioning air spaces between them. Typically, the particles should measure 3–12mm ($1/8$–$1/2$in). The depth should be 30cm (12in) and it will need raking to maintain the depth.

Unless your ground is very well drained you should install a free-draining base of hardcore or coarse gravel to a depth of about 15cm (6in) and lay this to a fall to take the excess water away. To stop the safety surface mixing with the base you can put a geotextile membrane between the layers. Let it settle and then top up as necessary. You will probably need to edge the area to contain the surface.

# PROJECT: A DOUBLE SWING

Even if you have only one child, a double swing is worth the extra effort when friends come to play. The rustic frame of this design helps it blend into the garden and tough climbers may be established to incorporate the play structure still further.

## PRACTICAL TIPS FOR SAFETY

Site the swing carefully, making sure that it is not positioned where passers-by are likely to be hit by an enthusiastic swinger. A safety surface of bark, rounded particle sand or rounded particle gravel laid over a length of 2.5m (8ft 3in) in front of and behind the seat and to the width of the swing frame provides a good soft landing.

Fit a rubber safety seat (see Suppliers, page 166). A swing seat is hung with the rope at an inside angle of 85° to prevent the seat swinging from side to side, and knocking into the adjacent swinger or a side post.

## BUILDING THE SWING

### The legs

First prepare the poles for the legs. Do this by laying each pair of leg poles on the ground in the shape of an 'X'. The poles should cross about 500mm (20in) from their tops (the thinner ends) making an angle of approximately 46°. This angle is produced by having the centre line of the poles 1.95m (76¾in) apart at a point measured 2.5m (98½in) down each leg from the centre point where the poles cross.

Mark the area where each pole overlaps and cut this portion away to form a flat-notched face about 20mm (¾in) deep. Now lay the leg poles in pairs to form crosses, with their notched faces together. Support the uppermost pole at the end furthermost from the

## YOU WILL NEED

- Four tanalized, peeled rustic poles, 3.85m (12ft 8in) long, 100–150mm (4–6in) in diameter, to form two pairs of 'legs'
- Two supporting side poles, 3.9m (12ft 10in) long, 100–150mm (4–6in) in diameter
- One tanalized, peeled rustic cross pole, a maximum of 3.7m (12ft 2in) long, 100–150mm (4–6in) in diameter. Use the thicker dimension if the children are heavy.
- Concrete, 1:6 mix cement : ballast, 0.75 cubic metre (1 cubic yard)
- One barrowload of free-draining granular material
- Two ready-made rubber safety swing seats, such as a belt seat which comes with metal rings to attach the rope to, a flat rubber safety seat which also requires four eyebolts M10 (10mm/⅜in) diameter with 25mm (1in) shank and nut or a single tier, or a rubber cradle seat, which comes with a metal ring to attach the rope to

- Synthetic rope with a breaking strength of ½ ton, approximately 12m (40ft) in length (note that, if swing chains are used instead of ropes, they require suitable bearing assemblies to fix to eyebolts)
- Four eyebolts M10 (10mm/⅜in) diameter, with shanks 125–175mm (5–7in) long, depending on the pole thickness, the eye to be of sufficient size to take the rope
- Coach bolts with protective coating, M10 (10mm/⅜in) diameter, of length to suit poles, with single coil washers, washers and nuts:
    two to join leg poles, 200–300mm (8–12in) long;
    four to attach cross pole, 240–340mm (9½–13½in) long.
- Two wooden connectors, size to suit poles
- Round wire nails, galvanized 150mm (6in) long

### Tools

Saw • Chisel • Spade • Shovel • Hammer • Drill • Spanner • Plumb-line • String lines and pins

joint so that it is parallel to the ground and then drill a hole through the joint to take the coachbolt. Fix the bolt using a wooden connector between the posts, and a plain washer and a single coil washer before the nut. Tighten the nuts.

### The cross pole

Mark the approximate point where the cross pole is to be bolted to the leg poles, and mark the approximate positions for the eye bolts according to the drawing. Drill holes to take the eye bolts, in a straight line and through the axis of the pole; this is important to avoid weakening the cross pole. Fix the bolts using a large plain washer, then a single coil washer, before the nut.

### Preparing the ground

Mark out the position of the four leg poles and

then the two side poles. For 100mm (4in) diameter poles, dig rectangular holes, 600 x 350mm (24 x 14in); for 150mm (6in) diameter poles, extend the width of the holes to 400mm (16in). Dig the holes 850mm (34in) deep; place 50mm (2in) of free draining hardcore or coarse gravel in the base of each hole and firm it down.

### Positioning the leg poles

Stand the leg poles in the holes and stretch a string line along the centre axis of the holes on each side. Use a plumb-line to make sure that each joint is vertically above a point halfway along the axis. Support with a batten nailed temporarily in position and, finally, check along the pairs of poles that the inner 'faces' just straddle the axis (see illustration).

### Securing the cross pole

Next, lift the cross pole into place with the

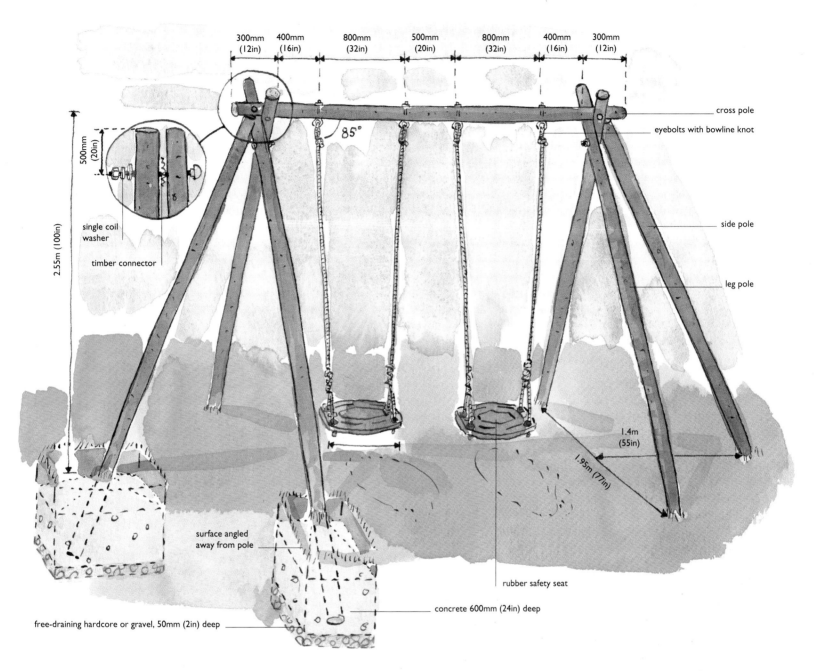

300mm (12in)  400mm (16in)  800mm (32in)  500mm (20in)  800mm (32in)  400mm (16in)  300mm (12in)

85°

2.55m (100in)

500mm (20in)

single coil washer

timber connector

cross pole

eyebolts with bowline knot

side pole

leg pole

1.4m (55in)

1.95m (77in)

surface angled away from pole

rubber safety seat

concrete 600mm (24in) deep

free-draining hardcore or gravel, 50mm (2in) deep

eyebolts hanging vertically. For security, tie the ends of the cross pole into place temporarily, then drill holes through one end of the cross pole and the upper ends of the leg poles and bolt together, with the bolt heads downwards. Repeat for the other end. Tighten the bolts, using washers and single coil washers before the nuts to stop them unfastening.

## Securing the leg poles

Making sure that the poles are central in the holes, stand one of the side poles in its hole and mark the exact position where the top face meets the underside of the cross pole. Saw off the top of the side pole at an angle of approximately 60° then prop it in the hole. Skew nail the side pole securely into the cross pole and the nearest leg pole, with 150mm (6in) galvanized round wire nails. Repeat for the other side pole.

Ram concrete into the holes to within 200mm (8in) of the top and smooth it so that the concrete is angled away from the poles. Leave the concrete to set for 48–72 hours.

## Hanging the swing

Fix the eyebolts and hang the swing seats at the required height, using synthetic rope. Hang the rope at an inside angle of 85° to ensure that it swings straight. Knot the rope firmly onto the eyebolt using a bowline knot *(see page 67)*.

### FINISHING AND CHECKING

Regularly check that the ropes are not starting to fray, that the wood is sound, that all the fixings are secure and for general wear and tear.

# PROJECT: A CLIMBING PERGOLA

This pergola/climbing frame is designed to provide a play structure which can be converted into a conventional pergola, providing a framework for climbing plants, when the children are older. Ensure that the siting of the pergola works in design terms both now and in the future. It might straddle a pathway leading to a focal point, for example. If you temporarily block off the pathway with a play feature such as a scramble net, then provide an alternative route in the short term.

## PERGOLA DESIGNS

The design shown on these pages may be adapted to suit different size gardens and situations. The basic unit is a pergola arch with six uprights. In most situations I favour a pergola formed from a series of archways, with definite gaps between them, as this style is usually more easily absorbed into the garden setting. Another advantage is that different archways can become different play features, perhaps one with a trapeze, another with a scramble net and so on. The highly visible archways could be treated as purely ornamental features and covered with climbers, and the less visible ones used for play. It is also possible to link a number of archways with horizontals to make a much larger structure. This will have great play value but is more difficult to integrate into a garden, particularly if the garden is small or informal.

## UNDERNEATH THE PERGOLA

The surface underneath the pergola should be a safety surface such as bark or gravel (*see page 60*). Gravel intermingled with plants may well best complement the surrounding garden, unless perhaps your pergola leads through light

**YOU WILL NEED**

**for a double arch**
- 12 vertical posts, 100mm x 100mm x 2.9m (4in x 4in x 9ft 8in) tanalized softwood, planed all round
- Four horizontal front beams, 100mm x 100mm x 2.3m (4in x 4in x 7ft 8in) tanalized softwood, planed all round
- Two horizontal side beams, 100mm x 100mm x 4.5m (4in x 4in x 15ft) tanalized softwood, planed all round
- 10 ladder rungs, 38mm x 50mm x 1m (1½ x 2 x 40in) tanalized softwood, planed all round, free of knots
- Four ladder rungs, 38 x 50 x 550mm (1½ x 2 x 22in) tanalized softwood, planed all round, free of knots

- 20 coach bolts with protective coating 220mm (9in) long, M10 (10mm/⅜in) in diameter, with single coil-washers, washers and nuts
- Countersunk zinc plated no. 12 screws, 75mm (3in)
- Concrete, 1.25 cubic metres (1.6 cubic yards) 1:6 mix cement : ballast
- One barrow load of free-draining material
- Gravel to surface
- Non-toxic wood stain

**Tools**
- Hand saw • Spade • Shovel • Drill • Countersink bit • Spirit level • Spanner • Screwdriver • Hacksaw • Fine flat file • Plane • String lines and pins

woodland in which case bark chippings may be more appropriate. Always use rounded particle gravel, which does not interlock in the way that angular gravel does.

## BUILDING A PERGOLA
### The archway

Having decided where to site the pergola, mark out a rectangle 2.1 x 1m (84 x 40in) with crossed string lines. Four of the posts stand in the corners of the rectangle. The remaining two posts are centred between the corner posts on the short sides, making these three posts at 450mm (18in) centres. Dig out a trench for each set of three posts, 850mm (34in) deep by 1350 x 450mm (54 x 18in), centred on the short sides of the rectangle.

Next place a 50mm (2in) depth of free draining material in the base of each trench. Position the posts in the trenches and brace them with scrap wood so that they stay upright. Pour in the concrete to within 200mm (8in) of the top, checking again that the posts are vertical with a spirit level. Angle the surface of the concrete away from the posts to

drain away water. Leave the concrete to harden for 48–72 hours, then fill to ground level with gravel. Install the posts for the second archway in the same way, spaced 2.1m (84in) from the nearest posts of the first archway if you intend to link them with side beams.

### The horizontal side beams

Clamp or tie the 100mm x 100mm x 4.5m (4in x 4in x 15ft) horizontal side beams to the posts, or ask two helpers to support them in position, while you drill holes through the vertical posts and the beams to take the bolts. Fix each side beam with a bolt, washer, single coil washer and nut at each of its junctions with a vertical post, to link the two archways.

### The horizontal front beams

Position the horizontal front beams on top of the horizontal side beams as shown. Drill holes to take the bolts and then fix them with a bolt, washer, single coil washer and nut to the vertical post at each end. Next trim off the tops of the vertical posts, leaving about 50mm (2in) proud of the horizontal front beams.

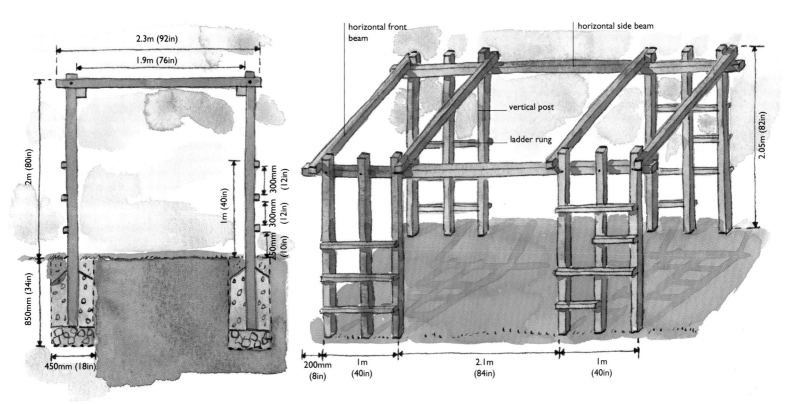

## The ladder rungs

The ladder rungs are fixed to the vertical posts with two countersunk 75mm (3in) screws at each station. Counterbore the holes so that the screw heads sit 6mm (¼in) below the surface. If the tops of the rungs are rounded they are easier for children to grip so, using a plane, create a smooth, gently rounded top on each one. The exact position of the rungs will depend on the particular feature that you are creating, but do not make them closer than 175mm (7in) or they may form a trap.

### TO FINISH

Cut off all protruding bolt threads flush with the nuts using a hacksaw. File the ends smooth and dab with enamel paint. Treat the wood with two coats of preservative wood stain.

### ADDITIONAL FEATURES

Attach rope ladders, a trapeze, a monkey swing, a scramble net, or a climbing rope. Take care to site a swing well away from other play elements in order to prevent accidents. It should be hung from one of the middle horizontal front beams, so that it is anchored in both directions, and fitted with a rubber safety seat.

### CLIMBING PLANTS

Site plants away from the areas used for climb-ing as the dead leaves could lead to damp, slip-pery surfaces. Recommended plants include the thornless, cerise pink, *Rosa* 'Zephirine Drouhin', which will even thrive on the north-facing side of the pergola; the white wisteria, *Wisteria venusta* and many of the honeysuck-les, which provide fragrant, sometimes ever-green, cover. Limit the selection to two or three species to give a strong, unified effect.

### REGULAR CHECKS

Finally, do not forget to check the pergola at least twice a year to make sure that it is struc-turally sound, that the wood is in good shape, and that the bolts and fixings are sound.

Single arch    Double arch with rope ladders and climbing pole    Double arch with scramble net and knotted ropes

*The single arch unit can be used alone* (left), *in a sequence of three or more, or joined to a second arch with horizontal beams* (centre and right).

# Informal Climbing Structures

If you do not have the space or the desire to have a conventional climbing frame in your garden, there are a number of alternatives which are often quite simple and inexpensive to construct. An added advantage of these more informal ideas is that they are less finished and more dynamic so that they change and develop with the child's imagination. For example, a well-positioned rope ladder hung from a suitable tree next to a clump of bamboo can be a fire engine's hoist one day and a ship's ladder the next.

### CLIMBING TREES

The most traditional and in many ways the most exciting garden feature to climb is a tree, which has the added benefit of fitting in easily with the planting of a garden. The ideal climbing tree will have spreading branches which swoop down to within easy reach of the ground. Apple trees often develop limbs which turn them into good climbing trees. Trees to avoid are those which have brittle branches such as *Robinia pseudoacacia* (false acacia) and any that develop dead wood. Even dead trees, if the wood is sound, may be turned into horizontal climbing features like the dragon below or set upright in concrete and turned into

tailor-made climbing frames with a few judiciously placed pegs (*see opposite*).

### HANGING ROPES FROM TREES

If the lower limbs of the tree are out of reach, a rope ladder, knotted rope or perhaps a purpose-made wooden ladder lashed to the tree can bridge the gap. You can set the height of the lowest rung to exclude younger children. The rope should be synthetic nylon or

*Large branches or tree trunks left to lie not only look decorative but also make wonderful climbing structures for children. They can be set to allow space beneath for dens and niches on top for seats. The dead wood also provides a rich habitat for wildlife.*

polypropylene (more durable than hemp), and should have a half-ton breaking strength; usually a 9–10mm (⅜in) diameter man-made rope will provide this. The most environmentally friendly colour is white which weathers or dirties to the attractive hemp colour. The commonly available orange and blue will jar uncomfortably against the natural colours of the garden.

### FIXING A ROPE TO A TREE

When you are fixing items such as a rope ladder, swing seat, trapeze bar, trapeze rings, twizzler, monkey swing or a rope to a branch, tie the rope (or ropes) securely to the branch

*This splendid carved dragon is the centrepiece of an infant-school playground. His large size enables several*

*groups of children to play together simultaneously, and he is ideal for inspiring fantasy games.*

*If you do manage to acquire an old log, make sure you maximize any*

*potential hidden identity that it possesses.*

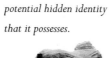

with a bowline knot (*fig 1*). Next throw the long end or ends over the branch. This is to make sure that the swing does not wear on the knot, but constantly wraps and unwraps itself around the branch (*fig 2*). Bark can be very abrasive so, before fixing the rope to the tree, check that the contact point is smooth. If you are fixing a plain rope, a large knot on the bottom is good for grip while climbing on and for sitting when swinging; use a double overhand knot for this (*fig 3*).

## SAFETY PRECAUTIONS

Always check at least once every six months, and preferably monthly, that the knots on any ropes are safe, and replace immediately any rope that starts to fray or show any sign of wear. Also check regularly that the branch is still able to support the load that it is required to carry (remembering that a child's weight increases yearly), that it is not rotting, and that any ropes used are not constricting the growth of the tree.

*This dead tree has been repositioned and anchored in the ground with concrete. The wood is regularly checked for signs of decay. Pegs have been fixed into sound wood at frequent intervals to facilitate climbing. When your children's climbing days are over, plant a honeysuckle or other climber (below) so the tree will blend successfully into the garden.*

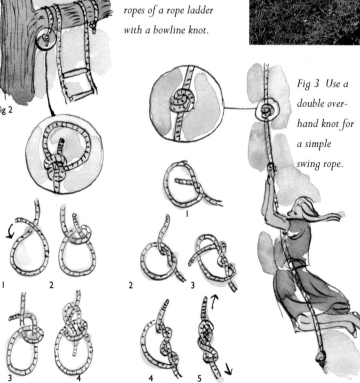

*Figs 1 and 2 Tie the ropes of a rope ladder with a bowline knot.*

fig 2

1  2  3  4

fig 1

*Fig 3 Use a double over-hand knot for a simple swing rope.*

1  2  3  4  5

fig 3

### Fixing Detail of Peg into Dead Tree

For climbing, you can set a dead tree trunk upright in concrete (obtain dead tree trunks from parks or sawmills). Check security of fixing and soundness of wood at least twice yearly. Have a maximum fall height of 2m (6½ft) and lay a safety surface.

❶ Saw off unsafe/badly placed branches (leave longer if they will carry a swing).
❷ Ensure the wood shows no decay.
❸ Drill holes 100mm (4in) deep to take 25–35mm (1–1⅜in) diameter dowels at suitable intervals for climbing.
❹ Saw off 300mm (1ft) lengths of ramin dowel; glue into the holes.
❺ Saw 50mm (2in) lengths from a 60mm (2½in) diameter dowel, round edges and glue to each peg to cap.

# Playing Ball

Whatever the age, sex and number of your children, it is likely that ball games of one sort or another are popular. If you can incorporate into your garden a flat area of lawn where, for example, badminton, rounders, softball or short tennis can be played it will pay big dividends. Depending on the space you have available, this area can have trees and mixed planting surrounding it, and maybe a table and chairs or banks and steps from which to watch play. The planting must be tough, established and up to the job, so that you do not have to cramp the players' style (which is often not easily done anyway). Bearing in mind the plants may be trampled in the search for a lost ball, use shrubs which will

*Rounders is an ideal game for larger family gatherings as younger players can join in too. The pitch size can be adapted according to the age of your players and the size of your garden, but you will need a fairly large stretch of lawn.*

## Table of Garden Games

| GAME | PITCH SIZE | COMMENTS |
|---|---|---|
| **Archery** | Target 46–91m (50–100yd) from archer | This is once again becoming a popular sport. |
| **Badminton** | 13.4 x 6.1m (44 x 20ft) | For 2–4 players. Site court in sheltered spot. |
| **Croquet** | 25.6 x 32m (28 x 35yd) | For 4, 6 or 8 players. Pitch size can be reduced if necessary. |
| **Clock golf** | Any size | For any number of players of all ages. |
| **Deck tennis** | 4.3 x 8.2m (14 x 27ft) | For 2–4 players. Ideal for windy situations. |
| **French cricket** | Any flat green space | For 2 or more players. An excellent game for the garden or beach. |
| **Golf** | A golf driving range net can be used in smaller gardens | The best way to practice drives. |
| **Horse shoes** | Two 1.8 x1.8m (6 x 6ft) boxes, placed 9–12m (30–40ft) apart | For 2–4 players. This game is commonly called quoits, not to be confused with deck tennis. |
| **Lawn tennis** | 23.8 x 11m (78 x 36ft) | For 2–4 players. Few gardens have the space for this. |
| **Palas** | No court. In a confined space, fix the ball to some elastic tied to a brick. | Any number of players. This game is popular in France and Germany. |
| **Quoits** | 4.3 x 8.2m (14 x 27ft) | See deck tennis. |
| **Rounders** | Pitch size approx. 12m (39ft) between posts | Reduce pitch size for younger players. |
| **Short tennis** | 13.4 x 6.1m (44 x 20ft) | For 2–4 players. Used to teach children tennis. |
| **Soccer** | Any flat green space will be used | Damage limitation needed. |
| **Table tennis** | Table 274 x 152cm (9 x 5ft) | For 2–4 players More enjoyable outside than in, provided it is not windy. |
| **Volleyball** | 1.5 x 9m (4 ft 11in x 29ft 6in) | Officially 6 players per side, but still an enjoyable game when played with fewer people and a smaller court. |

shoot back, such as *Cotoneaster* spp., *Kerria japonica*, *Rhus typhina* and buddlejas (see the Tough Plant Directory on page 150 and Barrier Plant Directory on page 153 for other ideas). Alternatively, limit play to the dormant season when the herbaceous plants are safe below ground.

Certain ball games can be played with no grass. Boules, or petanque, for example, is best on a rougher surface such as gravel, making the game less predictable and limiting the travel of the ball. Palas can be played on any surface and in very small spaces; you need only a wooden bat (similar to a table tennis bat) and a ball. There is no net, no court, and no rules. The aim is to keep the rallies going as long as possible, and the closer you stand the faster the play. Deck tennis, as the name implies, was invented for exercise on board ship, and can be played on gravel or other hard surfaces as long as you can fix the net posts in the ground. (Although gravel will give nasty grazes, rounded gravel is a shock-absorbing surface on which to fall.) A basketball net can be fixed in many convenient sites, and keeps children of a wide age range amused.

Tennis is highly popular, but few people have the space for the real thing. Short tennis,

a scaled-down version using softer balls and lighter racquets, can be played in the average garden. Alternatively, real enthusiasts can buy a semi-rigid high net with the net line marked on it which will return the balls, an excellent way to practise. A wooden wall also works well, but makes enough noise to upset neighbours as the ball pounds against it.

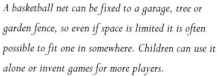

*A basketball net can be fixed to a garage, tree or garden fence, so even if space is limited it is often possible to fit one in somewhere. Children can use it alone or invent games for more players.*

Golf can take the form of clock golf or mini golf. Alternatively, to practise your drives you can use a specially designed light ball or a golf driving range net, though the latter is rather imposing for small gardens.

If you think your plants are more important than sport, balls on elastic for the children are the answer. You can obtain a baseball batting trainer set, a swing ball and circles tennis, none of which require a large area.

For those who are really short of space, outdoor table tennis in a sheltered position is practical. An inexpensive way of making a table is to fix a painted wooden top of the correct size over an old kitchen table.

*BELOW LEFT Here a rustic soccer goal has been designed to fit into some low box hedging, which protects the rough plants behind.*

*BELOW The ideal surface for boules is gravel. Shown here is a bound golden gravel, though the larger-particle loose gravel used for driveways would work.*

# Ball Games for Gardens

### SHORT TENNIS

Originally developed as an ideal pre-tennis training game, short tennis is an excellent garden game for all ages. The strokes and rules are all similar to lawn tennis but the rackets are smaller and lighter, the ball is softer and the court a lot smaller. The court size for short tennis is 13.4 x 6.1m (44 x 20ft) with a centre line for serving; there should be a minimum of 1.8m (6ft) space at either end of the court and 1.5m (5ft) at the sides. The net is 79cm (2ft 7in) high at the centre and 83cm (2ft 9in) at the posts.

### CLOCK GOLF

Clock golf can be played on any fairly level lawn – a circular one is not required and in fact a lawn of an unusual shape makes for a more skilful and interesting game. Design the clock face as large as required, make a hole in the centre, mark out the 12 numbers of the clock and put a flag and cup in the centre. The object is to pot the ball from each number. All you need is one ball and one club and the number and age of the players is limitless. If you feel more adventurous you could make your own mini golf course complete with obstacles such as bunkers, drainpipes, ramps and so on.

### BADMINTON

This is ideally suited to the garden lawn and there are no balls to inflict bruising. Two or four players can play at one time. The court measures 13.4 x 6.1m (44 x 20ft) and the net is 76cm (2ft 6in) deep; the top edge is 152cm (5ft) from the ground in the centre and 155cm (5ft 1in) at the posts. The rackets and shuttlecocks are relatively inexpensive, as are the posts and nets. The court needs careful siting as wind can disrupt play.

## FRENCH CRICKET

This simple, popular game can be enjoyed from three years old upwards. A cricket bat, baseball bat, or tennis racquet is used to shield the batsman's lower legs, while the other players try to get him out by hitting him below the knee with the ball. It is usually played with a tennis ball, as anything harder could be lethal. The rules vary, but are commonly that the batsman is out if a fieldsman catches the ball with both hands, or single-handedly with one bounce. The batsman clocks up runs by passing the bat around his legs in circles.

## DECK TENNIS / QUOITS

As the name suggests, this game was designed to be played on board ship and so is ideal for a smallish garden. A net 142cm (4ft 8in) high is strung centrally across a rectangular court measuring 4.3 x 8.2m (14 x 27ft). A 'neutral zone' which extends 45cm (18in) into the court on either side of the net is marked out. The game requires 2–4 players and a quoit (a small round rubber ring) which is thrown single-handedly across the net, caught single-handedly and then instantly returned from the same position. Points are won when your opponents fail to return the quoit into the court, and lost if it touches the ground in the neutral zone. When you reach 15 points you have won the set, and three or five sets are usual.

## SOCCER

This is among the most popular ball games, particularly for boys. Assuming you have some lawn, a goal carefully sited to minimize the impact on plants may well be very popular with some members of the family. A wooden frame with a natural-coloured netting fits in better with most gardens than an aluminium frame and orange net. If your garden is large enough, you could designate a specific patch and ensure that the planting around this area is sturdy; if your garden is restricted in size then the best solution may be to ban football when the herbaceous plants are above ground.

# Sand and Water

If you have ever watched the absorbed concentration with which children play with sand and water, you will not have the slightest doubt that they are, in some way, satisfying a basic need. Although public parks often provide sand pits and paddling pools for children, some of which are beautifully maintained, the attraction of having your own smaller version for everyday use is immense – for adults and children alike.

### THE PLEASURE OF SAND

Small children derive great pleasure from sand and it forms a safe play area, but even older children will become engrossed in creating sand villages – complete with turrets, moats and bridges – often entertaining younger children into the bargain. Sand provides children with an opportunity to experiment with a ma-terial which can be moulded, shaped, shov-elled, poured and stirred, and which can be wet, dry, heavy or light. While playing with sand, children start to learn basic physical concepts including volume, density and gravity.

### DESIGNING AND SITING A SAND PIT

Sand is inexpensive, readily available and, pro-viding the edge treatment of the sand pit fits in well with the surroundings, it will look at-tractive in most gardens. Even in the smallest garden, an area of sand which several children can play in together is a worthwhile invest-ment. While the children are very small, it is obviously useful to have the sand pit fairly close to the house, where it can be easily observed. However, keep it away from doorways as sand does have a habit of travelling. If you site the sand pit in a sunny position, you may need to provide umbrella shade in high summer. The dappled shade of a tree may be suitable if you are prepared to remove fallen leaves.

When you are designing and siting your sand pit, do not necessarily think of it in isola-tion, but consider combining it with other features that appeal to children so as to open up further spheres of play. For instance you could make a large, sunken sand pit, contained with log edging, and grow a willow tepee beside it, or even in it if you do not mind col-lecting dead leaves. Alternatively, a low seat and table made from simple log rounds form an ideal 'work station' for play.

### COMBINING SAND AND WATER

Sand and water complement one another for children's play. If you do not want to site a pool of water by the sand pit, a large refillable

*Sand play often triggers a great spirit of cooperation among children who will often work industriously together on projects building viaducts, tunnels and race tracks. The 'sand machine' illustrated here would greatly excite sand enthusiasts with its fantastic opportunities to weigh, balance, slide, haul, and generally wallow in the versatility of sand.*

*This drainable paddling pool combined with a wooden-edged sand pit is set flush with the ground. With lawn right up to the edge and a subtly coloured beige liner, the pool is well integrated into the garden.*

(line with a geotextile membrane), or a large, ornamental bowl or trough of some sort. Many manufacturers sell specially made plastic sand pits which are undoubtedly enjoyed by children but their brightly coloured finish is a bit of an eyesore in the garden. Better-looking are the ready made, raised timber sand pits — some are available with a small canopy over them and timber seats either side. These types are also easy to make at home, with planks forming the four sides and diagonal seats made across the corners. Alternatively, a sand pit could be made from an old up-turned table by fixing wooden planks across the legs to form raised sides and removing the lengths of leg that extend. It could be painted or stained to co-ordinate with other garden features.

## BUILDING A SAND PIT

If you decide to make your own sand pit, a good size is about 1.2m (4ft) square with the minimum size for small children to play in about 70cm (2ft 4in) square. If you choose to build it with raised edges, these should be approximately 38cm (15in) high, so that smaller children can clamber over them. The same measurements apply for the depth of the pit, if you decide to make a sunken one, but only fill a sunken sand pit to a depth of about 22cm (9in) to avoid losing too much sand over the edges.

### Laying the base

When you make the sand pit, whether it is raised or sunken, it must have a free-draining base, so that the sand has a chance to dry out. If it is permanently wet, bacteria, algae and similar undesirables will breed in it and turn

bowl or trough that suits the surroundings would contribute enormously to the play value of the sand. Add some pebbles and boulders which can form dams, walls and bridges.

## A FORMAL DESIGN

If you are siting the sand pit directly by the house a more formal solution, such as a sunken pit designed as part of the terrace using co-ordinated materials, may well be the most suitable answer. An ideal edge may be to partially surround the pit with raised walls, which could be wood, stone or brick, and about 30–40cm (1ft–1ft 4in) high to form additional

seating space and help to contain the sand which enthusiastic users inevitably hurl about with gay abandon. Leave a break in the wall so that any travelling sand can be easily swept back in at the end of the day's play. Of course the day will come when the children stop using the sand pit, and then the sunken area can be filled in with plants, paved, or made into a small water feature.

## SIMPLE SOLUTIONS

If you really do not have the space or the inclination to build a larger sand pit, the simple solutions are containers such as a tractor tyre it sour. One method for adequate drainage is to lay old paving slabs over the base with 1cm (⅓in) gaps between them. If you are on extremely free-draining soil, it is possible just to place a layer of geotextile membrane over the base of the pit, and put the sand directly on top of this. The membrane allows drainage, but stops earthworms, moles and creepy-crawlies ranging freely and mixing the sand with the soil.

If your soil is not well drained, and you have no old paving slabs, then put in a 5–10cm (2–4in) deep layer of free-draining hardcore or gravel over the base, laid to a fall. Blind the hardcore if necessary with some sand to form a smoothish top, then lay the geotextile membrane with the sand on top. If your garden is permanently wet with a high water table, then you have three choices: the first is to put in drainage; the second is to opt for the above-ground sand-pit; and the third is to change the sand regularly.

### Filling the sand pit
When you come to fill the sand pit, make sure you use the sand sold especially for sand pits.

*This small sand pit was carved from local weathered stone which complements the house so well that its prominent siting on a terrace outside the kitchen window does not detract from the atmosphere of the garden. This is an ideal sand pit solution for young children.*

Sand sold for this purpose is now classified as a toy and so must satisfy certain criteria. Play sand is a light-coloured sand, which means it does not stain clothes, it is lime-free, and has been washed and graded. Building sand is not suitable, as it stains clothes and, when wet, can form a yellow sludge – not good for high quality sand castles. Play sand is available from many toy shops and builders' merchants in small, easy-to-carry bags. If you want a large quantity, you can order it from a builders' merchant in loose loads, or in very large sacks.

### Suitable coverings
Having filled your sand pit with this wonderful, tactile medium, you really should provide a cover to prevent the local fauna using it for their less attractive purposes. The design of the cover must be in keeping with the pit and it should not be solid, as exposure to air and sunlight keeps the sand sweet. An attractive and relatively easy-to-make cover can be formed from strips of wood and the webbing roll widely available from garden centres where it is sold by the metre or yard. The roll is made from light strips of wood laid side by side with gaps in between, linked by two or more webbing bands stapled along the top. This flexible cover is easy to move, even for children. Alternatively, stretch bird or chicken netting over the top of the sand pit.

### PADDLING POOLS
Paddling pools are the traditional way of providing for water play in the garden and, if you are looking for an alternative to the ready-

*I designed this paddling pool and sand pit to look like a natural brook. The pebbles are laid on concrete and form the waterproof base to the drainable paddling pool. The pool is cleaned out each year and chlorine is added during the summer months. The planting is protected by horizontal logs.*

made plastic variety, a more permanent and attractive form to make is illustrated on pages 78–79. However, water for play can be incorporated into the scheme in many other ways.

If you are lucky enough to have a well, an old-fashioned hand pump which gushes on to an area of slightly dished paving forms a delightful play feature. Alternatively, make a small, dished pool out of concrete to hold pebbles, shells and sparkling clean water. The pool could be filled with a hose and drained through a plug hole. An adjoining stretch of pebbles, shingle and sand would provide complimentary additions for play.

Even simpler options include a large bowl, old sink or waterproofed wooden barrel cut in half. Any of these, positioned under a tap and surrounded with boulders and shingle, will provide excellent play value.

*LEFT Instead of trying to hide or disguise a sand pit, this delightful boat design illustrates how to turn it into a garden feature which provides a positive contribution to the garden. There are fabric 'sails' which provide a partial sunshade for the occupants during high summer. RIGHT A water channel made from granite setts has a water supply and is drainable. When not in use for sailing boats and cooling feet, it is emptied and forms a decorative surrounding to a paved area. Designed and built by Roger Storr.*

# Sand Pit Edging

*Note: for all five designs, the sand is laid over a geotextile membrane which, in turn, is laid over a 5–10cm (2–4in) depth of free-draining, blinded hardcore or coarse gravel.*

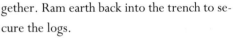

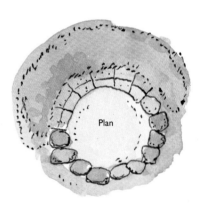

Plan

Section

### A CIRCLE OF LOGS

This surround is made from a ring of sawn logs which are set into the ground. If you do not have suitable logs, tree surgery companies will often supply cut-down tree parts or, failing that, try a saw mill. A suitable log ranges in size from about 20cm (8in) to 30cm (12in) in diameter. Set the logs into a trench about 30cm (12in) deep, butting them closely together. Ram earth back into the trench to secure the logs.

### GRASS BENCH

The grass bench surround has been made from turves, laid turf side uppermost in the same way that you would lay bricks in a wall. Cut turves about 5–10cm (2–4in) thick and lay the first layer on to the soil platform building up the bench in layers until it is 10cm (4in) below the lawn surface. This should be carried out in the autumn or spring, and the turves should be well watered until the top turves become established. The grass will form a vertical green wall fairly quickly, which will need to be trimmed with shears to keep it short. To protect against constant trampling of the banks, reinforce some of the walls with a tougher material such as logs.

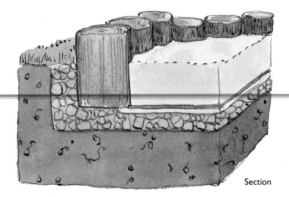

Section

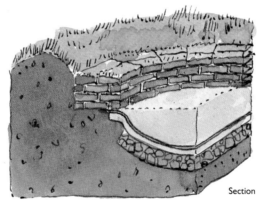

Plan

### BOULDERS

If you have access to a supply of smoothly rounded boulders, they can be used to form an attractive margin to a sand pit. Ideal for sitting on, they also form an interesting, irregular edge with crevices for play. It will be impossible to mow closely around the backs, so leave a mowing margin of about 15cm (6in) wide filling it with a suitable material such as cockle shells. If natural boulders cannot be found, it is possible to make reasonable substitutes out of concrete. First, in an unused part of the garden, dig a boulder-shaped hole and line with polythene. Next, make a mix of concrete and tint it with an appropriate colouring compound. Pour into soil mould and leave to harden (48–72 hours).

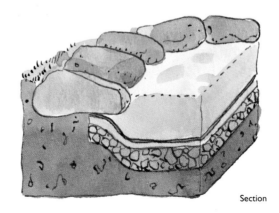

Section

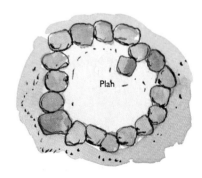

Plan

## MINI AMPHITHEATRE

If you have an existing, shallow dell in your garden you could construct this mini amphitheatre from stepped logs. The logs are about 30cm (1ft) long by a similar width. The bottom level of logs is set into the base of the slope on the free-draining surface, fixed with a metal reinforcing bar through each log (drill the log first) and driven into the ground to a depth of about 50cm (20in). The middle level is set into the slope, with the logs joined together with metal staples or skew nailing. The

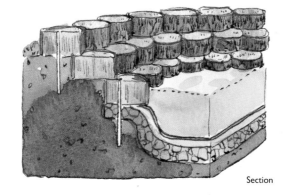

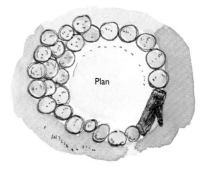

Plan

Section

top layer is also fixed with metal bars driven into the ground in the same way as for the

bottom layer. Check that the structure is safe and secure.

## WILLOWS

Here a living screen fence of willows has been set on a mounded bank to provide a secluded sand-pit-cum-den with a beach dune feel. To make this feature, form a gentle mound around the proposed sand pit using the soil that was excavated to make the sunken sand pit. Replace the soil you have removed with free-draining hardcore or gravel base before laying the geotextile membrane and sand. Next, make the screen fence by taking slim branches about 2cm (¾in) in diameter from a vigorous willow such as *Salix alba* during the dormant season, and push them into the soil mound to a depth of about 30cm (12in), leaving vari-

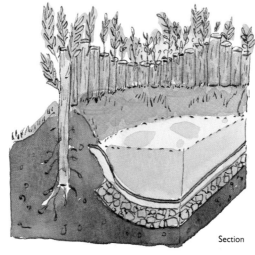

Section

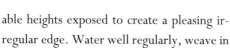

Plan

able heights exposed to create a pleasing irregular edge. Water well regularly, weave in

new growths to fill out the walls and trim them to the required height.

**KEY**

Top layer of sand

Geotextile membrane

Free-draining hardcore
5–10cm (2–4in) deep

*Once established, the willow edging develops into a dense, bushy screen providing a very secluded sand pit. The small bank into which the willow cuttings are set prevents excessive sand loss in the early stages.*

# PROJECT: A PADDLING POOL

This small paddling pool, which is constructed using a heavy gauge butyl liner and is flush with the ground, is filled from the hosepipe and has a drain allowing it to be emptied and cleaned periodically. The size of 1.5 x 1.5m (5 x 5ft) by 450mm (18in) deep can obviously be varied according to your needs. Whatever the depth, make sure that the children are watched while the pool is in use, as it is possible to drown in less than 150mm (6in) of water. Butyl does puncture, so treat it with respect. When the pool is not being used, put a protective safety cover over it, anchored in position, rather than leaving it empty and vulnerable to falling debris, curious animals and the like.

## YOU WILL NEED

- Heavy duty butyl liner 3.5 x 3.5m (11ft 6in x 11ft 6in) for the size of the pool shown here; available in black, blue or stone colour (the stone colour is recommended)
- Underlay, of the same area as above
- Weak mortar mix 1:1:8 (cement : lime : building sand) 0.3 cubic metre (0.4 cubic yard) for lining pool.
- Free-draining gravel or hardcore, 0.6 cubic metre (0.8 cubic yard)
- uPVC threaded tank connector, 50mm (2in) (see *Suppliers, page 168*)
- Universal plug, 100mm (4in) in diameter, to cover tank connector
- uPVC waste pipe, 50mm (2in) in diameter; length depends on position of soakaway
- uPVC 90° elbow, 50mm (2in)
- uPVC stop valve, 50mm (2in)
- uPVC soil pipe, 1m (33in) by 100mm (4in) in diameter.
- Access cover for soil pipe
- Concrete, 1:6 mix (cement : ballast), 0.4 cubic metre (0.5 cubic yard)
- Mortar, 1:5 mix (cement : building sand) for paving
- Mastic sealant
- Solvent cement for uPVC
- 12 paving slabs, 450 x 450mm (18 x 18in)
- 4 paving slabs, 450 x 600mm (18 x 24in)

## Tools
- Spade • Shovel • Pickaxe • Club hammer • Steel float • Spirit level • Stanley knife • Scissors • Hacksaw • Half-round file • Large spanner

## BUILDING A PADDLING POOL
### Digging out the pool

First dig out the pool itself to 150mm (6in) below the required final level of the base. Make the sides of the pool about 10° off the vertical – 100mm (4in) further in at the base in a 600mm (24in) deep excavation.

From the centre of the base dig a trench for the drainage pipe 150mm (6in) wide by 100mm (4in) deep to the edge of the pool base, then continue through the sidewall to the position of the proposed soakaway or drain. Be careful not to undercut the sides, to avoid any danger of them collapsing. If you are connecting it to an existing ditch or drainage system, then the required fall will be governed by this; otherwise the fall can be minimal, as the weight of water alone will drain the pool. To make a soakaway, dig out a small area at the end of the trench about 600mm (24in) square to a depth of 900mm (36in) below ground level.

### The drainage

The pool is drained through a 50mm (2in) diameter uPVC tank connector, fitted in the trench at the centre of the pool base. It is controlled by a stop valve positioned a convenient distance away from the pool. You will find it easier to assemble the pipework outside the pool because of the access problems of doing so *in situ*. Attach a 90° elbow to the bottom of the tank connector and run 50mm (2in) uPVC pipe from the elbow to the stop valve. Connect a second length from the valve to the soakaway, to finish 300mm (12in) into the soakaway. Lay the assembled pipework in the trench, and prop the tank connector in position vertically so that the top is flush with the final base level of the pool.

To allow access to the stop valve for draining the pool, cut a length of 100mm (4in) diameter uPVC soil pipe to fit over and around the valve. Cut a notch in the bottom end so that the pipe straddles the drainage pipe and

sits on the bottom of the trench. Place a suitable cover over the top, which should be just below ground level, to prevent feet getting caught in it and to maintain a level base to the pool.

### Back-filling

Prop a board over the end of the trench at the soakaway to contain the soil, then back-fill the trench, compacting the soil firmly to the contour of the disturbed side wall. Level off the soil inside the pool flush with the excavated base. Fill the soakaway with free-draining hardcore to within 200mm (8in) of ground level then top up with soil to ground level.

### Preparing the base and surround

The next stage is to excavate foundations for the paving slabs around the top of the pool. First cover the tank connector, to keep out debris then excavate to a depth of 225mm (9in) below the base of the slabs.

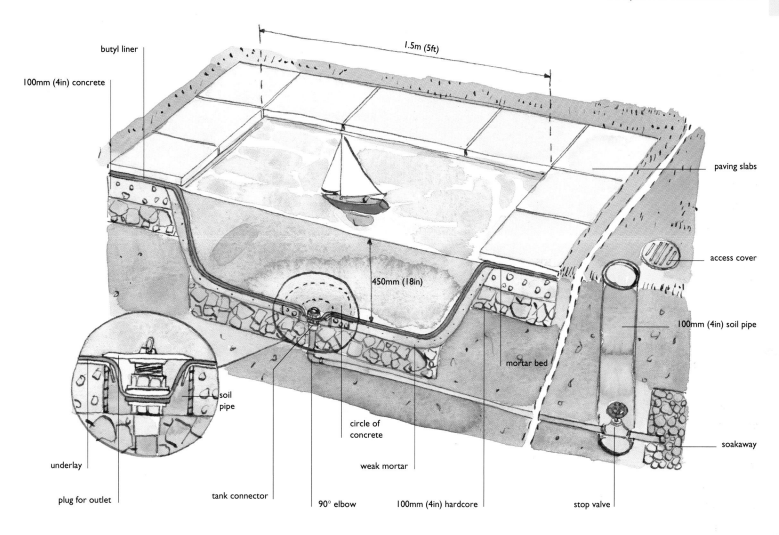

butyl liner

100mm (4in) concrete

1.5m (5ft)

paving slabs

access cover

450mm (18in)

100mm (4in) soil pipe

mortar bed

soil pipe

underlay

plug for outlet

tank connector

circle of concrete

weak mortar

90° elbow

100mm (4in) hardcore

stop valve

soakaway

Lay 100mm (4in) of well compacted gravel or hardcore over the entire base of the pool, leaving 50mm (2in) of the tank connector exposed. Cut a 50mm (2in) length of the soil pipe and fit it centrally around the connector, to act as shuttering, then lay a 300mm (12in) diameter circle of 1:6 mix concrete, 50mm (2in) thick, around the protruding connector. Level the concrete with the top of the tank connector, checking with a spirit level.

Lay a firm base of hardcore 100mm (4in) thick over the ledges for the slabs, followed by a 100mm (4in) bed of 1:6 mix concrete; prop 100mm (4in) boards above the hardcore, angled to the slope of the walls, to contain the concrete. Check concrete is level with a spirit level then leave all concrete to set for 48–72 hours.

Cover the base of the pool all around the concrete surround to the tank connector with a 50mm (2in) thick layer of weak mortar mix and trowel the same mix up the pool walls. Weak mortar is more stable than sand alone; it will prevent indentations from children's feet forming in the base and hold in place over the walls when the pool is emptied.

### Fitting the liner

First remove the top nut and washer of the tank connector. Next fit the underlay, covering the base and sides of the pool and the paving slab foundations. Cut a small hole around the top of the tank connector and tuck in the underlay around it. Lay the liner over the underlay, working from one side. At the centre of the base, cut a hole just smaller than the tank connector. Apply mastic sealant to the bottom nut and washer, and to the underside of the liner at this point, then stretch the liner gently over the top of the tank connector and

on to the washer. Apply more mastic to the top of the liner and to the top washer and nut, position the washer, then screw on the nut tightly to seal the liner to the tank connector. Lay the liner over the rest of the pool, gathering it neatly into definite folds rather than leaving lots of small creases. Find a suitable plug, such as a large universal sink plug, to sit inside the top of the tank connector and cover the outer pipe (it need not make a watertight seal).

### Laying the surround

Lay the paving slabs over the liner on a continuous bed of 1:5 mix mortar, 25mm (1in) thick. They should overhang the pool by 20mm (¾in), and be horizontal and completely level with each other. When the mortar has set (48–72 hours) the pool can be filled.

# OUTDOOR LIVING

*A well-planned garden should be at the hub of family life, providing an attractive setting for a host of memorable occasions including birthday teas, picnics, informal barbecues and summer siestas. On top of all this, it can also fulfil the oldest role of a garden — as a supplier of food for the family. Today there are countless vegetable varieties to maximize yield and flavour while many are attractive enough to add visual appeal as well.*

# Eating and Entertaining

Eating outdoors is an almost unbeatable pleasure in a warm and sheltered spot, surrounded by luxuriant foliage and a colourful haze of blossom, with a little dappled shade throwing a pattern across your plate. The informality of these outdoor events makes them particularly suitable for entertaining guests of all ages. Accidental spillages matter much less, children can come and go and in the case of barbecues everyone helps with the cooking.

However, eating outdoors can also be utterly unenjoyable if the environment is not right. We have all experienced problems of one kind or another whether it be gusts of wind blowing food off the table, sizzling in the sun on a sea of red hot paving with wasps driving you crazy, or being watched by the neighbours as an all-out family battle rages.

### THE PERFECT SITE

Make unhappy outdoor eating a thing of the past by investing some care and thought in siting the eating area. The main attribute for a good outdoor eating area is shelter from the wind and a warm, sunny spot. This will vastly affect how often you will be able to eat outside. Often the most convenient place to eat in the garden is directly outside French windows leading to a kitchen; this has obvious advantages for ferrying food to and fro. If you have not got a conveniently positioned door, do seriously consider adding one, as the ideal entrance to the ideal spot will greatly increase your enjoyment of eating in the garden.

However, directly outside the kitchen may not be the best place for an eating area. For

*ABOVE I designed this small sheltered eating area to look as though it was sited in a ruined building. The wall is constructed from rendered concrete blocks, finished with pieces of brick and stonework and painted Tuscan pink. LEFT The late John Coddrington designed this space from some dilapidated farm buildings. The old mangers now form well planted containers, a new 'window' in the end wall frames a delightful view and interesting tubs add finishing touches.*

example, there may be a more sheltered site further into the garden where there are no eddying gusts. Perhaps being deeper in the garden this site will also be more lush and tranquil and provide some privacy.

The style of enclosure chosen for the outdoor dining room provides much of its individual character. A variety of ideas for enclosures are pictured on these pages and include an orchard setting, the remains of a farm building and a specially made garden wall designed to look like part of a ruin made good.

*This orchard eating area is very simple and delightfully shaded and leafy. It belongs to a large family whose numbers frequently swell with visiting friends. A sheltered glade is provided by fruit trees creating an effect which is charmingly informal, lush and green. The table was made by the owner, Peter Farrell, from a single, huge plank of wood from a saw mill, with timber poles screwed to the underside.*

These structures form the framework, providing the shelter and privacy that makes the outdoor eating area successful.

### RINGING THE CHANGES

If space allows, it is a great luxury to have a choice of eating areas for different times of the day and for different wind conditions. Another option is to designate a small area for everyday eating and a larger area for entertaining a number of guests. These outdoor eating areas tend to become the hub of the garden providing a focal point for family life in much the same way that a large kitchen does in a house, so it will rarely be a wasted allocation of space.

## IMPROVING THE SITE

If wind or sun is a problem and you cannot move your eating area, bear in mind that you can alter the microclimate dramatically in a short space of time. For example, our every-day eating area is small – just 4m (11ft) square and is on the north side of the house, on top of a hill, and therefore exposed to unceasing south-westerly winds. It is there because it is directly beside the kitchen French windows. More often than not in the summer, the family spills out for breakfast, elevenses, lunch, tea and supper. Surprisingly, the sun is not blocked out as that part of the house is a single storey and, during the summer months, most of the area is in the sun. Despite its unpropitious aspect and elevation, the area has been made even more comfortable by planting a series of windbreaks, including hedges, trees, a willow hurdle fence and some large mallows

(these last provide an almost instantaneous effect). We have another larger area, in a part of the garden which is almost always totally sheltered, which we use when the numbers swell or on exceptionally windy days. It is not

*BELOW LEFT This delightful covered area projects from the front door to a small eating area at the end. It spans the driveway and so helps to screen the view of the garage from the house. It was designed by Honor Gibbs for her own house.*

*BELOW CENTRE This small trellis pavilion was designed and built by Peter Farrell for his own garden. It not only encloses a small formal eating area but also frames a pleasant view down to his orchard.*

*BELOW RIGHT A large white parasol completely transforms this eating area giving it a luxurious colonial feel. Moveable shade is very practical when eating outside as it can be set up to take advantage of cooling breezes and minimize cold draughts.*

as convenient, but it does make a change to appreciate a different part of the garden.

It is also possible, of course, to design a single eating area to accommodate larger numbers if required so that, if the numbers do swell unexpectedly, everyone can be absorbed without massive upheavals. Extra seating can be provided by wide, shallow steps, perhaps with removable cushions. Walls of a suitable height are also invaluable to seat extra guests, whether they form the edge of a raised bed or are free-standing.

## A DINING ROOM OUTDOORS

It can be very successful to design your eating area as an outdoor dining room, partly enclosed by walls, a trellis, hedging, shrubs or masonry. Consider adding a partial roof for shade. This could be a light, overhead timber structure, a trellis adorned with climbers, a

boldly striped awning fixed to the house or just a simple umbrella. Furnish the 'room' with bold collections of pots to add interest, colour and focal points allowing the table and chairs to provide the main focus of the room. If the convenience factor of having a permanent barbecue appeals to you, and you decide to include it in the area, do make sure that it enhances the area and does not dominate it. The sight and sound of water adds another dimension to the eating area, and it may well

*How much easier and enjoyable life becomes when children can entertain their friends outside! No need to worry about the carpets and no doubt a feast will be provided for the bird and mammal population too! This simple log table with chairs is easy to make, ideal for a small garden and makes an attractive addition to any informal garden corner.*

make sense to position a water feature where it will be appreciated frequently. It is also then ideally sited to cool the wine!

## LIGHTING

If the eating area is to be used as an outdoor room, it is necessary to provide lighting so that it can be used in the evening. General illumination can be achieved by siting a lamp high up on an adjacent wall and this will allow you to move around safely and see what you are eating. More atmospheric effects result from spotlighting particular features or plants; the lights are generally sited low down so that they shine up at the chosen feature.

# Design of the Terrace

The terrace or main paved area in a garden is, more often than not, next to the house. It is a bridge between the house and garden and often acts as a visual tie linking the two spaces.

When you start to design the terrace area, the priority is to decide what character it should have and, in order to create a visual link, it makes sense that the style, scale and materials for the terrace complement the character of the house.

### DECIDING ON SIZE

The size of the house governs the size of the terrace area. A tall, imposing house makes a small area of paving look a little ridiculous so, in this instance, it pays to make the paved area proportionally wide as well as long. To avoid creating a wasteland of paving on a large terrace, the design could divide the area with patterns. A pattern might, for example, be laid in line with door and/or window openings.

If you have a small house, a proportionally small terrace is perfectly in keeping. However, if you have a tiny house, a very generous paved area is extremely useful and, so long as the large area of paving is broken up into smaller areas with a pattern, it can still look in harmony with the house.

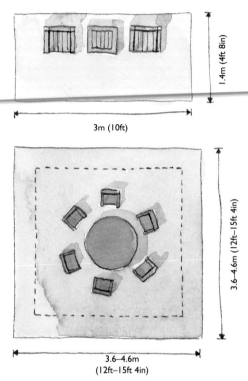

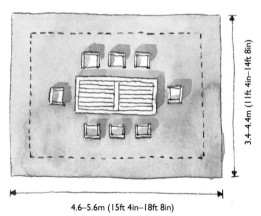

*It is important to allow sufficient space on the terrace to eat comfortably. The top illustration shows the minimum space required for a small table and two chairs on a terrace backed by a wall. The middle illustration shows the minimum and optimum area required by a round table which seats six (eight for an intimate meal). The bottom illustration shows the minimum and optimum area required to seat eight, or at a pinch ten people around a rectangular table.*

*ABOVE This terrace has been sited in a convenient, sheltered spot adjacent to the house and is further enclosed by high stone walls creating an enticing and highly usable tiny courtyard. The paving has been kept simple by the use of York stone slabs, but the generous planting creates a well-balanced, colourful space.*

When deciding on the size of the terrace, do not be too restrained. An attractive, highly functional family garden needs a good-sized paved area. It will probably be highly visible all year round, and usable for at least six months of the year. Work out the area required for the garden furniture and leave generous amounts of clearance around access points. Then decide where you are going to position borders and plants. The potentially difficult zone is the junction between the house and the paving. Almost invariably, this looks better as a broad border which will soften the edge of the house and help bind it to the garden.

## PAVING IDEAS

Paving is one of the most costly features of a garden, but cheaper forms of cover, such as bound or loose gravel, may be combined with more expensive hard materials. Areas of planting can also be used to form patterns within the hard area. An attractive chequer-board effect terrace can be created by alternating squares of paving with squares of *Sagina glabra*. In the most used areas, such as those with chairs and tables, a covering of paving alone is more convenient.

Another idea is to combine paved areas with small squares of grass to form regular patterns. The patterns can look stunning and the grassy areas soften the overall effect. Alternatively, lay paving with 20mm (¾in) joints leaving out whole slabs in places and planting and/or gravelling the joints and gaps with one or more varieties of very low-growing plants, *Thymus serpyllum* 'Snowdrift', for example.

## THE FINAL EFFECT

When you first view your newly completed paved area, it might look fairly big and barren. However, once furnished with plants which will overlap the edges, with garden furniture and containers, the character of the terrace will become apparent and the significance of the paving will reduce dramatically.

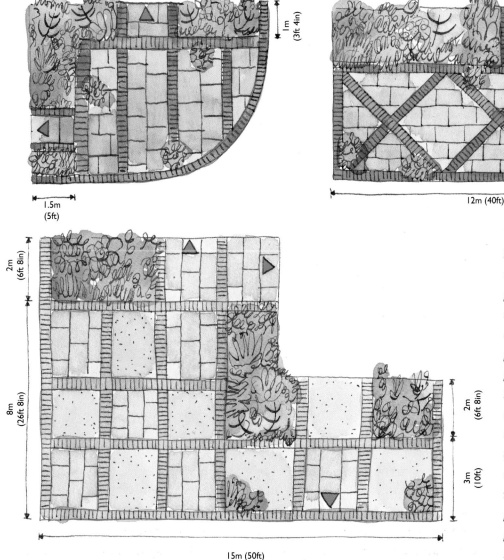

1m (3ft 4in)

1.5m (5ft)

2m (6ft 8in)

4.5m (15ft)

12m (40ft)

2m (6ft 8in)

8m (26ft 8in)

2m (6ft 8in)

3m (10ft)

15m (50ft)

*When designing the layout of your main paved area, bear in mind that it may well be the most used and visible part of the garden. There are some basic principles which apply: do not skimp on the size but make a good, usable space; avoid large, unbroken areas of paving by introducing a pattern; relate the scale and positioning of architectural details of the house in the paving patterns; avoid a run of paving going up to the house; plant generous borders between the house and terrace to link house and garden. The illustrations put these principles into practice: a small corner terrace (top left) is made to look larger with the strong vertical lines of brickwork; a wide strip of terrace (top right) is broken up and given interest with a criss-cross pattern; a large terrace area (below) is broken up by planting squares and by using a range of paving materials in a repeating pattern.*

### CHOICE OF PAVING MATERIALS

When selecting materials, perhaps the most important consideration is that the paved areas near the house complement the house materials and that they re-affirm the overall character you are aiming for.

### Gravel

Gravel is the least expensive hard ground cover and can be used to good effect. Edge the gravelled area with a generous band of paving slabs, brick or granite setts (the gravel will need to be swept back regularly) to prevent the gravel being taken indoors on shoes.

### Bound gravel

Bound gravel has a lot of very small particles which, when watered and rolled, compact it into a firm surface, which is less likely to be carried into the house on shoes and is also suitable for wheelchairs.

### Wood

Using timber for paving introduces a totally individual character. Options include diagonally laid decking combined with boulders for a modern, almost Japanese, feel, or log rounds placed vertically to give a network of uniform or variably sized circles. The logs should be a hardwood as the wearing properties of a softwood in this situation are not good. Fill the gaps between the logs with a green carpeter such as the splendid *Soleirolia soleirolii* (babies' tears) and/or bark mulch for a woodland feel, or crushed cockle shells and sand for a more exotic, jungle look. Old railway sleepers may be used to create a range of decking effects inexpensively.

### Stone slabs

This can be an expensive choice, although there are excellent reproduction stone paving slabs which are more economical. These are also easier to lay than real stone slabs as they are of uniform depth. Real stone slabs evoke a traditional feel and complement many other materials.

### Granite setts

Small unit paving materials such as granite setts are ideal if you want to make a small area of paving look bigger. Granite setts are available in green, pink, grey and white tones of granite and are a wonderful way of introducing patterns, such as bands or curves.

### Bricks

Bricks are usually laid in herringbone, basket weave or stretcher bond. They can be laid on

flat, that is with their wider face exposed, or on edge, which is less economical, but often looks better. All bricks must be of a suitable quality for paving, otherwise they will shatter in heavy frosts.

## Pebbles

Pebble paving and mosaics have a special charm with their colour variation allowing both abstract and figurative patterns to be made. Pebbles are also useful as a deterrent paving, to stop people cutting corners and walking too close to planting.

## Roof tiles

Laid on edge in blocks, circles or bands, the small unit size of a roof tile makes it suitable for a wide range of patterned effects; well used, roof tiles also make a small area look bigger.

## Terracotta tiles

With their rustic charm and warm pink colour, terracotta tiles can make a paved area look very much like an outside room. Treat with linseed oil and then paint with a waterproof sealant to improve frost tolerance.

## PRACTICAL CONSIDERATIONS

Do not forget to lay your paving to falls, which ensures that rain water is tipped away from your house. When designing a pattern, bear in mind that the most accomplished results generally incorporate an edge pattern of some sort. Also make sure that, where the paving butts up against turved areas, the turf is 15mm (⅝in) or so proud of the paving. This allows the lawn mower to run easily over the edge of the paving, leaving a clean, tidy edge, without wrecking the blades.

*OPPOSITE LEFT Gravel is one of the least expensive and most versatile materials ideally suited to the fluidity of informal settings and associating well with other hard landscaping materials in more formal situations.*
*OPPOSITE CENTRE These small paving units are extremely flexible: they can be used to form curves and informal meanders as well as geometric shapes.*
*OPPOSITE RIGHT This is a bound gravel surface edged with stone slabs giving a practical, inexpensive and attractive finish to a large area of terrace.*
*ABOVE LEFT A combination of bricks laid flat, pebbles and stone slabs create an intricate pattern. Pebbles are useful for filling odd-shaped gaps.*
*ABOVE CENTRE Brick paving is laid in a herringbone pattern with the bricks laid on their sides.*
*ABOVE RIGHT Characterful old stone setts have been laid with gravel for this enticing path. The stone setts are smooth on the top surface only and usually 10–15cm (4–6in) deep, so they are awkward to lay.*

## MAKING THE MOST OF STEPS

Steps provide an interesting link between house and terrace, or terrace and garden, and should be exploited to the full. They may be wide and grand, with deep treads and shallow risers, climbing the slope gently, or they may be very steep, narrow and winding, arousing curiosity. Alternatively, they may be quite simple, perhaps constructed from wooden treads with ivy or a low-growing cotoneaster forming the vertical riser.

When organizing the levels of a terrace, avoid a single step, as it tends to become a hazard. Make sure that the treads of the steps slope slightly to drain off water so that they do not become slippery.

## CONTAINERS ON STEPS

Basic steps can be transformed by lining the edges with potted plants. Containers are also useful for increasing or decreasing the visual height of steps, a bank or a wall. A high plant-

ing, perhaps in a tall container sited at the top of the steps, in conjunction with a very low planting at the base makes the change in level look particularly dramatic. To reduce the impact of a slope, reverse this by putting the high planting and pots at the base and very low planting at the top.

## CONTAINERS FOR THE TERRACE

The clever use of containers adds another dimension to any part of the paved area, bringing many possibilities. They are also fun to collect, especially as a diverse, eclectic collection often works well – rarely does a collection of dissimilar pots look bitty and fragmented. There is plenty of scope for serendipity when acquiring containers. My eyes recently lighted upon a disused, galvanized iron plasterer's bath, which is now embellishing my vegetable garden, draped with nasturtiums and *Lysimachia nummularia* 'Aurea' (creeping jenny).

## INCREASED PLANTING OPTIONS

Containers can also increase the range of plants you can grow in the garden. Plants such as bananas and citrus fruits can be moved outdoors in the warmer months and brought in to a kinder climate in the cold periods. They allow you to create soil conditions which you may not have in the garden – for example, an acid growing medium that will encourage rhododendrons to thrive. Container plantings are also a useful source of mobile colour, allowing you to introduce spots of intense colour created by flowers at their peak to a patch which is otherwise past its best.

## CONTAINER PLANTINGS FOR CHILDREN

Children appreciate the small scale of planting that a container provides and should be encouraged to create their own small container planting. A 40cm- (16in-) high pot is at a convenient height for a young child and large enough to provide some scope for planting. My six-year-old planted one with leeks and a red cabbage which did far better than those in the vegetable garden.

## PLANT MAINTENANCE

The drawback with plants in containers is the amount of time it takes to keep them in good condition throughout the summer months. If you are a busy, infrequent, family gardener, make sure that you insert a semi-automatic watering system inside the pots before the hot weather begins. This consists of a plastic container with wicks leading up from it which is placed on free-draining material in the base of the pot. The pot is then filled with loamless compost as usual and the tank filled with water through a tube that pokes up through the surface. In hot conditions, this will keep the plants moist for two weeks or so depending on what is being grown. The watering system comes with a dip stick so that you can

*Wood can work particularly well in informal gardens, and has been used here to build seats, decking and shallow steps which are adjacent to informal water.*

*The area has an inviting, relaxed feel about it, which encourages use. It was designed by Honor Gibbs, a landscape architect, for her own garden.*

check how much water is left in the container. For some reason these are rarely sold in garden centres, but they are available through specialist suppliers *(see page 166)*.

Alternatively, limit the pot inhabitants to those plants that flourish in minimal moisture situations (those that in their natural habitat tolerate drought are obviously well-suited). In my experience, plants such as box, yucca, agaves, and the chusan palm will put up with irregular watering care. Add a few groups of bulbs, such as tulips, that thrive on a good baking and the scene will be both attractive and undemanding of maintenance.

Most proprietary composts should contain sufficient nutrients for healthy growth, however, at the height of the growing season it may be necessary to supplement this once a week with some liquid fertilizer used according to the manufacturer's instructions.

*ABOVE LEFT These steps have been planted up with a wonderful assortment of abundantly planted pots which serve to highlight the steps making them appear much more dramatic than if they were unadorned.*

*FROM TOP RIGHT Beside a group of containers on a terrace is often an appropriate place to site a garden ornament or sculpture such as this child-orientated example. Finding the right site is one of the important aspects of using statuary in the garden.*

*This exquisite cactus collection belongs to a young plantaholic, and shows what you can do in a tiny space! Cacti appeal to children with their range of fantastic forms and their occasional stunning blooms.*

*A shallow sink has been raised right out of the ordinary by supporting it on two matching pieces of carved stone. These shallow sinks are easier to find and less expensive than deep ones.*

*Pots often come into their own when they are massed together to form a bold group, and an arrangement such as this transforms the dullest terrrace.*

# Barbecues

Whether you want to knock up an impromptu snack for the family or cook for a party, a barbecue can be a simple, no-fuss way to produce delicious food. The fresh air, the delicious aromas and the easy-going atmosphere that invariably pervades the occasion guarantee that a good time will be had by all generations.

There is no doubt that if you have a permanent structure to cook on outside you will use it more frequently than one that has to be set up for the occasion. Most of the portable ones are not objects of beauty and I would once have said the same about built-in structures because I had seen so many designs that would only have been presentable if completely covered with ivy. Now I have had a change of mind, and am convinced that built-in barbe-

cues can sometimes even enhance a garden. If you do decide to build one, choose a site that is convenient for the transportation of food and blend the barbecue into the surroundings with planting and pots so that it does not dominate the area.

### PERMANENT BARBECUE

Some of the most effective barbecues are in a recess in the house wall, but obviously this is only feasible in new buildings where they can be planned in. One particularly good example I have seen is constructed in the wall of a

*This well-designed stainless steel barbecue folds up into a portable cylindrical case, ideal for picnics or at home. When opened out the cooking area is generous as both sides of the cylinder can be used. It can also be used to smoke food.*

*This barbecue built from reclaimed bricks to match the existing wall has useful flat surfaces on either side for food preparation and spacious areas beneath for stacking items. If you burn wood you will get considerably more soot staining on the wall than if you only use charcoal. The bricks used for the fire bed must be of a suitable quality as some will explode when exposed to intense heat.*

*LEFT This old stone trough barbecue is dual-purpose. For cooking, two bars are screwed into sockets in the wall to support the grill tray. At other times it forms an attractive raised surface useful for sowing or potting.*

*BELOW The construction of the barbecue is straightforward, though you will probably need to commission a blacksmith to produce the grill tray and the threaded metal sockets in the wall which take the metal bars.*

new stone farmhouse. The barbecue rack sits on a pivoting bar that is simply screwed into a socket when you want to use it.

As with any feature, ensure your barbecue fits in with its surroundings. If it is beside the building, use the same material, be it brick, stone or render, and keep the detailing in tune with that around it.

My barbecue is an old stone sink which sits on two stone piers against the wall of the house, also stone. When not in use its true function as a barbecue is not apparent as there are several other similar sinks nearby which I use for washing vegetables and re-potting plants. The only difference is that in the wall are two pairs of threaded sockets into which you screw threaded bars before lighting up, and these bars support the grill. I put a layer of thin fire bricks on the base of the sink, as stone can crack or spit under intense heat. A shelf at the back keeps any smoke off the wall, but when using charcoal, as we do, this is not

usually a problem. A good way to make a compact heat source is to light the fire in an old galvanized bucket with the bottom knocked out and then gently remove the bucket when the fire gets going.

If you wish to build a stone sink barbecue against a cavity insulated wall it is advisable to support the grill tray by a different system, such as bricks on either side, as heat transference through the wall via the metal bars could be a fire hazard. Against a brick wall, use matching brick piers.

### TEMPORARY BARBECUES

Children are always fascinated by fires, and making a well-supervised temporary barbecue will bring them a good deal of pleasure; a few bricks or any suitable materials to hand will suffice. If they can cook food they have provided for themselves, such as sweetcorn they have picked from the vegetable patch, it will add to the illusion of a camping trip.

### HOW TO MAKE A STONE SINK BARBECUE

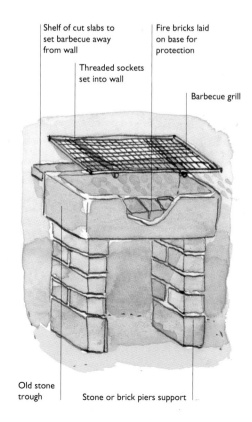

Shelf of cut slabs to set barbecue away from wall

Fire bricks laid on base for protection

Threaded sockets set into wall

Barbecue grill

Old stone trough

Stone or brick piers support

# PROJECT: A BARBECUE

The barbecue can be free-standing, or it can be built against an existing wall so that the integrated back wall can be omitted. However, if you are considering building it against an existing wall, bear in mind that the wall will become stained with soot.

## THE BRICKWORK

If the barbecue is to be built against an existing wall, the bricks should ideally match those already used. Ensure that the new brickwork courses line up with the existing brickwork and tie the barbecue walls to the back wall by screwing angle ties to it every other course above ground. Some bricks explode when exposed to intense heat, so avoid making the fire too close to the edges of the barbecue.

## BUILDING THE FOUNDATION

Using a builder's square, mark out on the ground where the walls are to be built. First mark where the centre of the walls will be and then expand these lines outwards by 260mm (10½in) on either side for the 215mm (8½in) thick brickwork, and 150mm (6in) on either side for the 102mm (4in) thick brickwork of the back wall. Dig this area to a depth of 450mm (18in). Work carefully and keep the sides of the trench neat and vertical.

Shovel in 150mm (6in) of a 1:6 concrete mix (cement:ballast), then level with the help of a length of wood and a spirit level. Once the concrete has set (allow 48 hours), lay four courses of bricks below ground using a 1:4 (cement:soft sand) mortar.

## LAYING THE BRICKWORK

Lay the brickwork using a string line to ensure straightness, and a spirit level to ensure that the bricks are perfectly horizontal and ver-

tical. The mortar mix above ground is 1:1:6 (cement:lime:soft sand). The 215mm (8½in) thick side and centre walls are five courses high, and built using English bond. This consists of alternate courses of headers (bricks laid across the wall thickness) and stretchers (bricks laid lengthways). You will need to cut bricks at both ends of each course to maintain the bond pattern and to bond in the back wall (see illustration). The back wall is 102mm (4in) thick and built using stretcher or running bond (bricks laid lengthways and overlapping half a brick length in alternate courses). The side walls are built to accommodate the two paving slab sizes used in the design, so check your brickwork against your paving slabs as you progress, bearing in mind that some reproduction stone slabs have irregular sides.

The sixth course on the side and centre walls changes to 102mm (4in) thick, leaving a ledge to support the two slabs. It is built in stretcher bond, and is again bonded into the back wall. The coping on one side wall and the rear walls is a half brick on edge.

When the mortar has set, lay one 600 x 900mm (24 x 36in) paving slab and the 600 x 600mm (24 x 24in) slab on top of the 215mm (8½in) thick side and centre walls as shown,

bedding them on a 1:4 mortar bed. Make sure that the slabs are very securely positioned, with a small gap of about 10mm (⅜in) between them and the back wall. Next lay the second 600 x 900mm (24 x 36in) paving slab on top of the two 102mm (4in) thick walls without a coping. Finally, backfill the foundation trenches with soil up to ground level.

## FITTING THE TRAYS

When the brickwork has dried out, it can be drilled and fitted with metal lugs in the ninth, tenth and eleventh courses above ground level to take the brazier tray and grill tray. The trays could possibly be made up by a local blacksmith. The former should be made of 16 gauge mild steel with 12mm (½in) holes drilled as shown and should have a raised lip all around the edges. Measure the exact opening once the walls are built, to ensure a good fit. The grill tray can be made from 3mm (⅛in) size welded mesh, with a frame of mild steel strips welded around the edge and braced in the middle. It is important not to make the fire directly on the concrete slab as concrete can spit or even explode when heated to high temperatures. For this reason, the brazier tray is housed almost three courses above the slab.

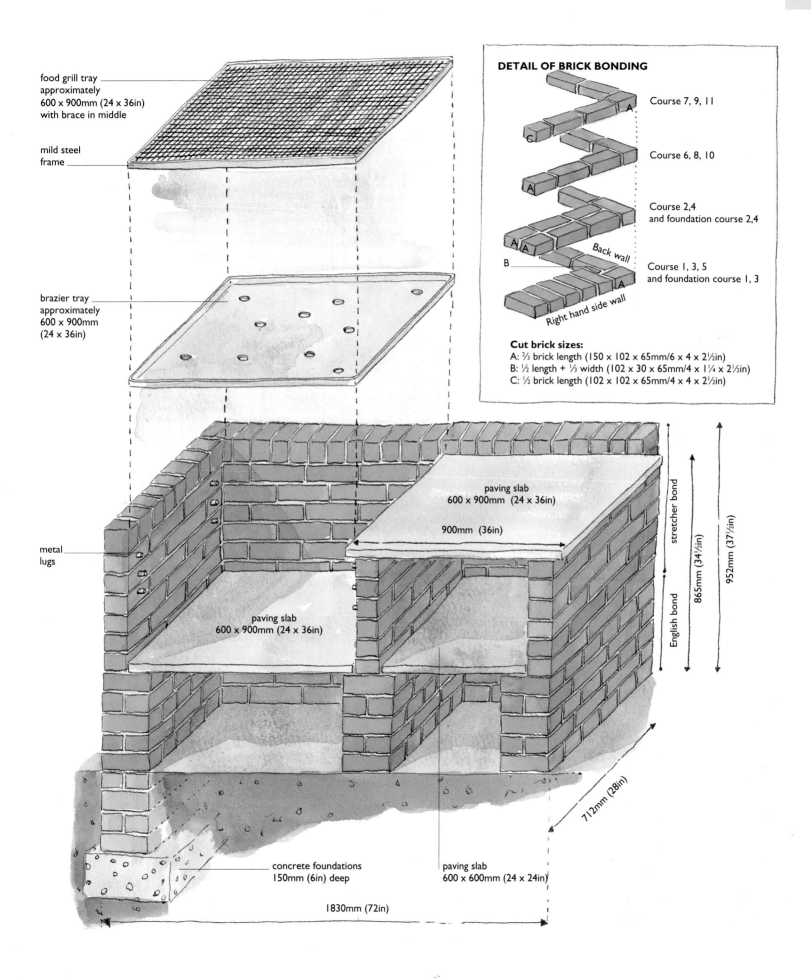

food grill tray approximately 600 x 900mm (24 x 36in) with brace in middle

mild steel frame

brazier tray approximately 600 x 900mm (24 x 36in)

metal lugs

**DETAIL OF BRICK BONDING**

Course 7, 9, 11

Course 6, 8, 10

Course 2,4 and foundation course 2,4

Back wall

Course 1, 3, 5 and foundation course 1, 3

Right hand side wall

A

C

A

A

A

B

A

**Cut brick sizes:**
A: ⅔ brick length (150 x 102 x 65mm/6 x 4 x 2½in)
B: ½ length + ⅓ width (102 x 30 x 65mm/4 x 1¼ x 2½in)
C: ½ brick length (102 x 102 x 65mm/4 x 4 x 2½in)

paving slab
600 x 900mm (24 x 36in)

900mm (36in)

stretcher bond

English bond

865mm (34½in)

952mm (37½in)

paving slab
600 x 900mm (24 x 36in)

712mm (28in)

concrete foundations
150mm (6in) deep

paving slab
600 x 600mm (24 x 24in)

1830mm (72in)

# Food for the Family

As fewer and fewer people have the space or the time to devote large areas of the garden purely to vegetables and fruit, it is becoming increasingly popular to grow certain edible plants laid out in an ornamental fashion. In this way the productive garden does not have to be tucked away out of sight but can be shown off for all to see. This integration of attractive vegetables and flowers is known as potager gardening (or, in the USA, edible landscaping).

Perhaps the most famous example of a contemporary potager garden is at Villandry, in France. This garden, dating from the early twentieth century and measuring 1.2ha (3 acres), is on a very grand formal scale with gravel paths forming the bones of the geometric design. Productive vegetables and fruit account for the bulk of the plants, while the purely ornamental element is made up of dwarf box hedging, standard roses and blocks of flowers such as petunia, polyanthus and verbena among the vegetables.

## DECORATIVE VEGETABLES

You may not want to concentrate on vegetables but just pop a few that are attractive and easy to grow into gaps in your flower borders. Some of the faster-growing types can be treated rather like summer bedding, being sown or planted in a mixed border. A wigwam of runner beans of the variety 'Painted Lady', some yellow bush courgettes ('Golden Zucchini'), a group of 'Bull's Blood' beetroot with their glossy dark purple leaves or some ornamental kale such as 'Peacock Tails' would quickly fill an unwelcome gap as well as any flowery annual. Other ideal vegetables to dot among the flowers are ruby chard, seakale, globe artichokes and ornamental and purple cabbage. Ruby chard, which has intense dark red leaves, is a substitute for spinach but is less likely to go to seed in dry weather and in a mild winter is productive well into December; seakale is an extremely ornamental perennial which you grow from thongs, or root cuttings, available from specialists. Leave it to establish for a year before you pick it,

*ABOVE Children are usually attracted to the vegetable garden, where they can grow their favourite fruits, make a sly raid on the fresh peas, play with mud pies or feed up their pumpkins for the local show.*

and then pick only gently in the second year. Once established the plant is a marvel, difficult to kill, stunning in appearance and regarded by some as a delicacy to eat; a further bonus is the charm of the wonderful clay forcing jars with lids that you place over the plants when the shoots start to emerge in spring. The edible part is the white blanched shoot, cut in April and May.

The globe artichoke is another eye-catching architectural plant, very easy to grow from seed and most delicious. It will enrich any border for a few pennies a plant. If you can bear to forfeit the succulent heads, let some plants flower so you can admire the impressive thistle-like purple display.

Asparagus is going out of favour because of its extravagant demand for space. It is also out of step with today's desire for instant

*LEFT The productive garden can be a visual treat with its colourful pattern of enticing vegetables. It is always worth experimenting with different varieties and types to see which ones best suit you and your cultivation conditions.*

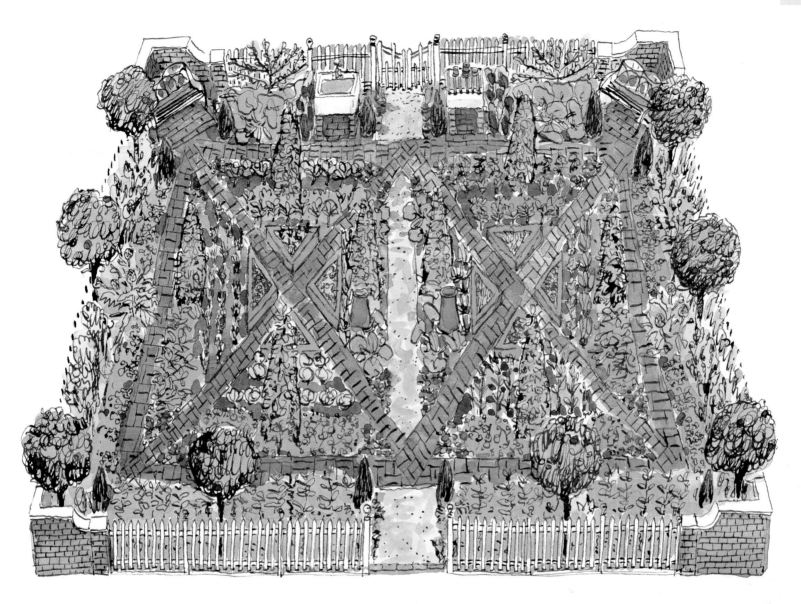

results, as it cannot be picked until it has been established for two growing seasons and then only lightly in the third year. Against this, new varieties are all male (which is to say productive), and so the yields have dramatically increased. If you do not want to devote a bed to asparagus, plant two or three large clumps in an accessible position in the border. The filigree foliage contrasts well with many other plants, such as peonies and irises and in autumn it colours up to a golden yellow.

## PROVIDING A FRAMEWORK

Vegetables you can train up canes will provide focal points in the border, the obvious one being the scarlet-flowered runner bean,

*The design and planting of this potager ensure that it will look attractive all year round. The patterns of the beds are reinforced in places with brick paving and low box hedging, while the palisade fencing provides extra interest. One stone sink allows preparation of produce while the other provides a convenient potting space.*

which will run up a bamboo wigwam with little or no help. There are also several unusual types of climbing French bean such as those with golden or purple pods, for example 'Gold Marie' and 'Purple Podded'. Pumpkins, gourds, climbing marrows and squashes can be trained up stout tripods if you want instant height; climbing nasturtiums can be mixed in with them for extra colour, and

the seeds will provide a caper substitute.

Winter colour and productivity can be lacking in vegetables, so if your potager is predominantly for the kitchen it helps to have an attractive permanent framework. A small area can be made interesting by dividing it up into a pattern of beds, traversed by narrow paths. These small beds are less daunting to work on as they are quickly transformed, and also they reduce the need to keep walking over the soil, thus compacting it and lowering the yields. Dwarf box hedges, fruit trees trained against arches, arbours or fences and topiary are ideal structural features, highlighting bed patterns to make the area look attractive even when there are no crops. Standard gooseberries are back in vogue, often grafted, though they can be simply trained from cuttings.

### WINTER VEGETABLES

A few vegetables are well worth while in the winter even for people with little time for gardening. Leeks are simple to grow and look good well into early spring, if you can spare them that long. The Jerusalem artichoke is a good standby for the long winter months as you can just leave it in place and dig it as you need it; it tastes delicious, but be warned that it is extremely invasive. Its tall stems provide an almost instant windbreak for the growing season and die right back in the winter.

There are many types of Chinese and Oriental greens and salads which may be lightly stir-fried or eaten raw; they have a spicy taste and many of them are aromatic. With a small range of these you may pick them fresh throughout the year, even in the winter months. One spicy, hardy one is a Chinese mustard called 'Gai Choy', or 'Green in Snow'.

The brassicas are a fairly common sight in the winter vegetable garden, but they are often under attack from many pests and so can be disappointing; maybe it's just the fact that it's not enjoyable tending them in miserable winter weather that makes them perform poorly on occasions. Nor does the taste differential between home-grown and bought seem so great as it is in some vegetables.

However, there are many other simple vegetables which look well slotted in patches in the flower garden. Broad beans, marrows, carrots, maize and endive are all easy, tasty and attractive. The 'cut and come again' lettuces are ideal for those who require a regular supply and dislike bare patches and regular sowings. A showy variety with frilly leaves is the red Lollo Rosso, which can be grown through the year. There is also a green and red 'Salad Bowl' which will last through the summer if picked regularly to prevent bolting. I favour the mixed Italian varieties such as *Misticanza saladini* 'Mesclun', which is trouble-free and can be broadcast in patches of the size required; if you want a spicy flavour add a pinch of salad rocket.

## Attractive and tasty vegetables

**Asparagus** A perennial vegetable with attractive ferny foliage which goes butter yellow in autumn; establish for two seasons from crowns (planted in the dormant season) before cutting. Likes free-draining soil.

**Artichoke (globe)** A wonderful, delicious, easy perennial vegetable which germinates well from seed. Sow seed in early spring.

**Artichoke (Jerusalem)** A rather invasive but extremely easy perennial which is an ideal plant for providing a fast-growing screen for other vegetables. Plant the tubers in the dormant season. Tubers to be used for eating can be dug up throughout the winter period.

**Beetroot 'Bull's Blood'** This variety has showy, glossy, dark purple leaves but does not form such big roots as less attractive varieties. Sow in mid-spring to early summer.

**Cardoon** These stunning perennials can easily be justified for decorative purposes only. If you want to eat them, treat them as annuals. In the autumn, earth them up and wrap up with straw or any other material which will exclude the light to blanch the stems, leaving only the tips of the leaves showing; three weeks later you can start to eat the blanched stems. They are easily grown from seed sown in early spring.

**Cauliflower 'Purple Queen'** A quick-growing purple-headed cauliflower for autumn; sow late spring to early summer.

**Climbing French beans 'Gold Marie'** A variety with pale yellow, flat, broad pods and white flowers. It is ideal for training up wigwams and fences. Sow mid-spring to early summer.

**Courgette 'Gold Rush'** A rich golden gourmet delight, forming a compact bush. Sow late spring to early summer.

**Cucumber 'Burpless Tasty Green'** An outdoor variety which is ideal for training up stout wigwams. Plant outside in early summer.

**Ornamental kale 'Peacock Tails'** The purple and crimson leaves make this plant really stand out. It is hardy through the winter, when the colour intensifies. Sow in early summer to plant out mid-summer.

**Ornamental cabbage F₁ 'Tokyo Mixed'** This is variegated in combinations of two to four colours of purple-pink, green and white, the colour intensifying through the winter. Sow early summer to plant out mid-summer.

**Lettuce 'Lollo Rosso'** An ideal cut-and-come-again lettuce with frilly red leaves. It can be grown throughout the year.

**Pumpkin 'Hundredweight'** This trailing pumpkin can be trained up stout canes to give height. It produces enormous yellow-skinned fruit. Sow seeds in late spring or early summer.

**Radicchio 'Variegata di Sottomarina Precoce'** The leaves are cut-and-come-again and can be eaten cooked or raw. When mature they are an attractive speckled red and white. Sow seeds in late spring to late summer.

**Runner beans 'Painted Lady'** This climbing bean has red and white flowers, splendid for tripods or wigwams. Sow in late spring or early summer.

**Chard 'Ruby Chard'** A variety with intensely coloured leaves of dark purple with a wide red succulent mid-rib. It is easy to grow and very hardy. Sow early spring to early summer.

**Seakale 'Superb'** An ornamental, simple-to-grow perennial. Sow seeds in early to mid-spring or plant thongs (root cuttings) in the dormant season, and allow to establish for 12 months prior to forcing with traditional clay seakale forcers or an old bucket.

**Squash 'Sunburst'** A bright yellow patty pan squash (a round squash with a scalloped edge). Plant out in early summer.

*Children will enjoy the bold colour effect created by*
Tagetes patula *(French marigold) and red cabbage. The*
*French marigolds will also attract beneficial insects*
*which will help to keep the vegetables in good health.*

## COMPANION PLANTING

The use of companion planting accords particularly well with this style of gardening.
*Tagetes patula* (French marigold) will attract
hoverflies, which feed on aphids, while nasturtiums secrete a substance into the soil which
is absorbed by plants and increases their
resistance to certain pests.

I prefer to grow my herbs in my small
potager rather than in a herb garden. French
or plain-leaved parsley, coriander, lovage,
mint, chives, basil, sorrel, tarragon and thyme
are in individual small squares surrounded by
low box hedging so that they can be covered
with fleece or glass through the cooler months.

*ABOVE Choose vegetables*
*according to the time*
*you can spend on them;*
*once your soil is weed-*
*free, many vegetables are*
*not labour-intensive.*
*LEFT Encourage young*
*children to garden by*
*giving them a small,*
*easy-to-work plot in a*
*part of the garden they*
*like. Start the very*
*young on plants which*
*give quick results.*

## PROVIDING GOOD SOIL

It is important to keep the soil in a productive
garden in good heart so that it is easy to work
and will produce healthy plants that will not
succumb to pests and diseases. If your soil is
on the heavy side, consider having raised beds
which can be worked without stepping on
them – a maximum width of 1.2m (4ft) by a
maximum length of 3m (10ft) is fairly standard. The sides are usually raised with timber
planks or old sleepers, although brick, if the
budget allows, can work well. If you do not
want to go to the trouble of supporting the
sides, you can slope them at the steepest
angle your soil will support. These slopes may
be left bare or planted up with low-growing
herbs that will appreciate the lack of moisture.
Make sure that the top edge of the bank forms
a slight ridge, so that when you irrigate the
top the water does not all run down the sides.
Raised beds can dramatically increase yields,
particularly in heavy soil, because of the reduced compaction and extra drainage.

# Garden Furniture

Garden furniture is a wonderfully versatile way of adding individuality to a garden design. Available in a vast array of styles, from traditional to modern, rustic, Regency, Victorian and Gothic, it sets the style of a garden simply and forcefully.

### USING COLOUR

Often, a simple, bold colour scheme for furniture is the most restful. Consider carrying the colour of the furniture through to other hard features such as fencing, gates and doors. To provide visual links, you could also paint some containers to match. If you want to make a seat into a focal point, a white painted finish offset by a dark green hedge will do the trick.

Blue is an underused colour in gardens which can work beautifully. Dark blue, bold blue, cornflower blue, turquoise-blue and grey-blue can be used to stunning effect on furniture, pots, and other paintable surfaces. Interestingly enough, these colours look good against brick and stone buildings, modern and old. It is worth trying to mix your own colours, or else buy antique shades.

For people who are not keen on the maintenance aspect of painted furniture, wood stains are an excellent option as the preparation process is easier. They are available in a wide range of colours, from bright reds, blues, greens, yellows to opaque white (which looks little different to a white paint finish).

### FABRIC EFFECTS

Colour can also be introduced to furniture with fabric – for example, a traditional, wooden deck chair with a bright yellow canvas seat makes a cheerful feature in the garden, or a swing seat draped in a boldly striped canvas cover adds a wonderful splash of colour and is very soothing to sit in. Cushions can also be used to emphasize the colour scheme. Awnings (over a terrace, for example) are another useful way to bring in colour, and can be co-ordinated with fabric on the furniture.

### USING INGENUITY

Almost invariably the most memorable pieces of furniture are purpose-made examples which

*ABOVE If you provide suitable outdoor sitting areas for young children outside, they will frequently use them for play as well as for eating, drinking and chatting.*
*OPPOSITE RIGHT Having created a wonderful garden, it is most important that you find time to put your feet up and admire it. So make it a top priority to find a really relaxing chair and keep it on hand for regular use.*
*OPPOSITE TOP LEFT This lovely old slatted seat has two lugs fitted on each metal side through which the supports to the canopy fit.*
*OPPOSITE CENTRE LEFT A simple set of well designed furniture creates an enticing seating area.*
*OPPOSITE BELOW LEFT An iroko seat forms an unusual focal point in this marvellous vegetable garden. The seat was designed and constructed by Nick Hodges.*

seem just right for their situation. This may be as simple as a curved bough from an old apple tree made into a simple, half-rounded bench, opportunely fitted around the base of a tree; or as sophisticated as a turf bench supported by bricks and built to form a raised rectangular seat with a clipped box hedge forming the back.

Two round stone balls with a long stone flag over the top make an unusual seat perfectly in keeping with many gardens, while an old church pew adds a characterful touch. Even logs can be fairly easily carved to form interesting shapes and simple seats. And do not forget the all-time favourite resting place – a hammock slung between two trees – which can be double or single and looks attractive both in and out of use.

### A FRAGRANT ARBOUR

To add a special finishing touch to any bench, enclose it in an arbour: three parallel hazel wands, each bent to form a wide arch is effective. Interweave short lengths of supple, green hazel into the arch to make it more rigid, then tie it securely with a natural coloured twine. Festoon it with a fragrant climber, such as an old rose, sweet peas or honeysuckle. If the hazel wands are not long enough, bind together short lengths to make the upright bones of the arch.

### CHILDREN'S FURNITURE

For small children's garden benches, upturned flower pots supporting wooden planks or treetrunk furniture (*see page 85*) are ideal. There is the additional bonus that they can be moved or grouped together as the children use the area for different activities.

# Unusual Garden Furniture

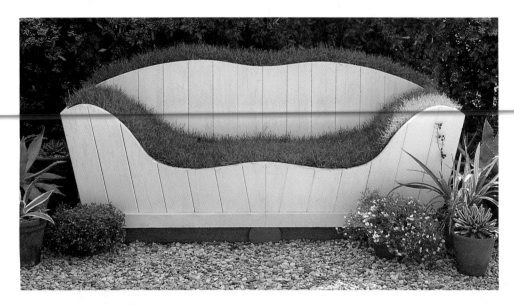

LEFT This eye-catching turf seat, ideally shaped for reclining, was designed by Dan Pearson. It is constructed from marine plywood faced with wooden boards, and there are drainage holes in the base to prevent waterlogging. The turf could be replaced with chamomile if you wanted to avoid the need for regular mowing with shears.

BELOW This small stone bench is an ideal children's seat, made from random rubble laid in courses with paving stones to sit on. It has only just been constructed, and alpine plants have been planted in small gaps in the stonework to contribute spots of colour in due course.

TOP LEFT Logs can be easily adapted to form comfortable and interesting seats, armchairs, benches and tables. They can be hollowed out in places to form containers for plants, and scrambling plants can be trained over them to add extra colour. If you take the bark off, the wood tends to last longer although it does not provide such a good habitat for insects and fungi.

RIGHT Hammocks must be the simplest and most romantic piece of garden furniture, and they can be enjoyed by all ages. They are made of cloth or rope, and may be single or double. If you are not fortunate enough to have two suitable trees they can be fixed to pergola beams, across a sunny corner of a building, or even between two climber-covered freestanding posts.

*The successful placing and styling of seats is dependent upon how you will use them. These two creeper-clad solid log chairs provide a place where two people can relax. Discovering suitable logs is not just serendipity: it also requires imagination!*

*LEFT On a scorching hot summer's afternoon the perfect spot to sit is underneath a tree in dappled shade, an ideal gathering place where five or more people can comfortably chat. Tree seats are often made with backs, making them a more comfortable and eye-catching feature, although you need a large, handsome tree to carry it off. Tables around trees can be charming too.*

# Garden Buildings

The commonest form of garden building is the garden shed. This is most frequently a prefabricated utilitarian building at the bottom of the garden and jam-packed with the lawnmower, old newspapers, tools and disused play equipment. These buildings are often best camouflaged with vigorous creepers, and indeed once they are totally covered they can look quite fetching.

If you are buying such a shed remember that it will not be possible to hide it from day one, so make sure you get one with a pitched roof as it is the roof line that makes many sheds look so unsightly. Paint or stain the walls to fit in with your garden. A subtle weathered olive green would help it harmonize with rampant climbers. Alternatively, you could make a statement by painting it with an eyecatching colour such as duck-egg blue, adding a few refinements such as a simple finial over the door and placing large pots of grasses outside.

The siting of your garden building will depend on the prominence you wish it to have. Whatever the building may be, the rules are to site it sympathetically, keep it in tune with the garden, do not be afraid to use colour boldly, and make it as usable as possible.

### MAKING YOUR OWN SHED

When you are looking for a suitable building it is easy to become overwhelmed by the range of styles available – and the costs. The best examples of garden buildings I have seen are invariably home-made or else especially designed to fit the site and the requirements. This is not necessarily the easiest option but it is generally much less expensive than buying one ready made and you really get what you want.

The overall style is the most crucial decision. Make sure that the character of the building you want will fit in with the garden, and that the colour and materials link in with those used nearby. Be cautious about siting it too prominently – buildings tend to blend in better when there is substantial foliage to anchor them to the garden.

Pay particular attention to the roof detail, as it often makes or breaks a building. If you cannot run to the luxury of handmade reclaimed tiles do not despair – consider cladding it with timber shingles, using an open trellis, thatching it or overlapping bands of stained plywood. The pitch and proportion of the roof are important – try drawing up different angles and sizes before you decide on the final version.

*BELOW LEFT This pretty 'New Jersey' pavilion is constructed from iroko with a moulded GRP roof. It can be obtained in a range of colour finishes.*
*BELOW CENTRE A summerhouse which forms the focus of the main sitting area. It can revolve, which means it can be directed to catch (or avoid) the sun.*
*BELOW RIGHT This modern building is adjacent to a pool and fountain. It is built of well-finished concrete and is on two levels linked by a spiral staircase.*

One of the best-looking garden buildings I have seen had a handmade lattice front and sides of irregularly shaped branches which were spliced and jointed together to form a rustic trellis. The arched doorway was made in the same way and there were curving wooden trunks for the front corners and a nondescript wall on the back. The roofing material was completely unobtrusive as it sloped away from the front, and the whole building was draped in white wisteria. Part of its charm lay in that it was unique, partially hidden, but extremely usable.

## GREENHOUSES

Greenhouses (or glasshouses, as professionals call them) are often eyesores, and as such are best hidden away. This is not easy as they obviously need the light, so cannot be lost among some big bushes like a shed. The best solution is to build one with a wooden frame (painted if you wish), which can last for a long time if properly treated. Design it so that it looks attractive perhaps with a base of stone or brick. Site the greenhouse with care remembering that they require regular attention so a bottom-of-the-garden position is not practical.

*LEFT This secluded thatched building in its wild setting forms a perfect hideaway and is a great draw to children as a centre for their adventures.*
*BELOW LEFT With modern technology, garden buildings such as this one can act as superb workshops, studios or offices. They provide a welcome retreat away from the family while still being conveniently close to home.*
*BELOW RIGHT This garden shed with greenhouse can function as a playhouse, a useful storage space and somewhere to sit and relax. It benefits from clever siting and generous planting and fencing.*

# THE WATER GARDEN

*It is rare to see a stunning garden that totally lacks*

*water in one form or other. Water adds a magical*

*quality to an outdoor space, and its diverse qualities*

*allow it to be used to create vastly different moods.*

*According to the nature of the garden, water can effect*

*a delightful transformation, be it a formal rill*

*contributing its refreshing coolness to a sunbaked*

*garden, a rushing, 'natural' stream adding speed and*

*excitement to an informal meadow or a stately*

*fountain providing a classical ambience.*

# The Appeal of Water

In the garden, a water feature exerts an almost magnetic pull on adults and children alike. The sound of running water and the visual delight of shallow sparkling water or deep limpid pools encourages us to become absorbed and our mood to become more serene. Interestingly, scientific studies have shown that the negative ions produced by moving water are conducive to a feeling of well-being in people and animals. Conversely, positive ions produced in hot windy desert conditions make people feel irritable and distracted, according to the same report.

## WATER FOR GARDENERS

From a gardener's point of view, water opens up new horizons, welcoming into the garden a different habitat with its own range of interesting plants, such as dramatic bog plants, floating water plants and a host of marginal aquatic plants. A water habitat also attracts many wild birds and animals of particular interest to children but fascinating for all ages. Ideally, site water where you can view it from the house. Although stark at first, a well-planted water feature can quickly look attractive and well established.

## CHILD SAFETY

Concern about including a water feature in a family garden is understandable. A baby or toddler can drown in the smallest depth of water required to cover his or her nostrils and mouth — a few centimetres. However, by including a safety grid in your pool, small children will be safe should an accident occur (babies and toddlers should be supervised at all times near water). The safety grid is a metal grille which sits about 5cm (2in) below the water surface, allowing water lilies and other water plants to grow through it so that it is scarcely visible. I banned my children from 'walking on the water' as they tended to damage the lily leaves, but visiting children unaware of house rules sometimes tried it without spills.

If you are still worried about the safety implications of having a pool in the garden, simple water features are safer still. For example, a bubble fountain makes a lovely focal point, or a shallow, racing rill of water running through a garden would be terrific for paddling and racing boats as well as providing a restful background sound. Even if you decide against a water feature initially, include one on your master plan to be added to the garden once the children are bigger.

*ABOVE Children adore stepping stones and will spend hours playing games on and around them. In butyl-lined pools, such as this one, they are constructed by placing additional underlay on top of the liner, on top of which a concrete base is placed to anchor the stepping stone.*

*OPPOSITE RIGHT By projecting the decking out over water, when you stand on it you almost feel afloat. It was designed by the landscape architect, Werner de Bock, for his own garden.*

*OPPOSITE TOP LEFT Small, shallow streams make ideal water forms for informal or wild parts of the garden. Do not forget the play element: leave parts of the water accessible, add a bridge or two and plant naturalistically to create a wilderness effect.*

*OPPOSITE CENTRE LEFT Bubble fountains bring in the attractive sound of running water to the garden and are perfect for the smallest plots. For added interest from water-loving plants surround a bubble fountain with a bog garden.*

*OPPOSITE BELOW LEFT Water is extremely adaptable and can make a great impact even on a small scale. A tiny water feature such as this will add a charming element to a corner and will also contribute to the play and wildlife value of a garden.*

# PROJECT: FORMAL AND INFORMAL POOLS

The formal pool has an edging of paving slabs, with one side raised above ground in the form of a low, brick wall – ideal for sitting on – and the other side flush with the ground. If you have small children, the raised edge provides a small safety barrier although both pools are fitted with safety grids. The informal pool is more natural with curved lines and soft edging with grass or planting.

The safety grid lies 50mm (2in) below the water level, so that water lilies and other water plants grow through the grid to help mask it. It consists of hollow section steel bars at 1.3m (51in) centres maximum, spanning up to 2m (79in) from one side to the other, with a metal grid fixed over the top. This allows the easy removal of the grid for thinning the vegetation and general maintenance. The grid is designed to take a loading of 22kg (50lb) mid-span, but do not allow children to play on it – it is not a play surface.

## A RAISED FORMAL POOL

### BUILDING A RAISED FORMAL POOL

The internal size of this pool is 2m (79in) wide by 3.06m (120½in) long. It is easy to adapt these measurements but, if you increase the width beyond 2m (79in), it will be necessary to increase the size of the square section steel bars accordingly (a simple calculation for a structural engineer). The length can be varied simply by changing the number of bars, bearing in mind they should be at a maximum of 1.3m (51in) centres, and the sheets of mesh should overlap by at least 100mm (4in).

### Setting out and digging the hole

Having set out the pool and established the proposed water level, start by digging the hole,

### YOU WILL NEED
**(for a formal pool)**

- 28 paving slabs, 450 x 450 x 38mm (18in x 18in x 1½in)
- Heavy gauge black butyl liner, 5 x 3.8m (16ft 6in x 12ft 6in)
- Underlay, 5 x 3.8m (16ft 6in x 12ft 6in)
- Additional underlay for underplanting and metal straps, approximately 4.2 x 3m (13ft 9in x 10ft)
- 90 bricks (those positioned at the water's edge must be of paving quality or similar)
- 32 dense concrete blocks, 100 x 225 x 450mm (4 x 9 x 18in)
- Building sand, 0.36 cubic metre (½ cubic yard)
- Concrete, 1:6 (cement : ballast) mix 1 cubic metre (1.3 cubic yard)
- Mortar, 1:4 cement : soft sand mix
- Four square section galvanized steel bars (made by a blacksmith), 1.85m (73in) in length, 20mm (¾in) square, with a 2.5mm (¹⁄₁₀in) wall thickness
- Specially shaped galvanized steel straps, 40mm (1½in) wide by 6mm (¼in) thick, to be welded to both ends (see illustration)
- Non-toxic black paint finish (for steel straps, above)
- Three galvanized steel mesh grids, 1.22 x 1.85m (48 x 73in), with 3mm (⅛in) diameter bars at 50mm (2in) centres, to be painted with a non-toxic black paint finish (The normal sheet size of mesh is 1.22 x 2.44m (48 x 96in). Ask a blacksmith to cut the sheet to the required size and smooth off all sharp ends)
- Galvanized wire for ties, 1.6mm (¹⁄₁₆in) thick (16 gauge)
- Reinforcing rods for concrete, 12m (40ft) in length, 10mm (⅜in) in diameter

### Tools

- Spade or digger • Brick chisel or bolster • Shovel
- Club hammer • Bricklayer's trowel • Spirit level
- Wire cutters • String line • Sharp knife or scissors

incorporating ledges as shown to accommodate marginal plants. The sides of the hole should slope outwards at about 20° (one unit outwards to every three up) to the vertical.

### Constructing the raised edge

Dig out the area which will form the edge treatment. If you are building a raised pool surround, excavate a trench 500mm (20in) below the finished ground level and 525mm (21in) wide. Fill the base of this trench to a depth of 225mm (9in) with 1:6 mix concrete. When it has set (allow 48–72 hours), build a 225mm (9in) thick inner wall of 100 x 225 x 450mm (4 x 9 x 18in) dense concrete blocks, alternate courses being laid flat as shown. Stagger the vertical joints in alternate courses by cutting the end flat blocks in half. The mortar mix is 1:4. The wall will be concealed

beneath the liner, so do not point it, but do rub off any projecting mortar to prevent damage to the liner. Build the wall to a height of 450mm (18in), putting in butterfly ties spaced at 900mm (36in) centres horizontally and 350mm (14in) centres vertically, to tie in the brickwork wall.

Next, build a 100mm (4in) thick brick wall. If preferred, you can substitute stone for the brick, but the facing stone would need to be 200mm (8in) thick and so the coping should be increased accordingly. This brick wall is in stretcher bond (with vertical joints staggered in alternate courses), eight courses high and is built on the concrete foundation and tied into the block work with the butterfly ties. Use the 1:4 mortar mix, and the wall should be pointed up. Keep the brickwork straight and vertical by using a string line and spirit level.

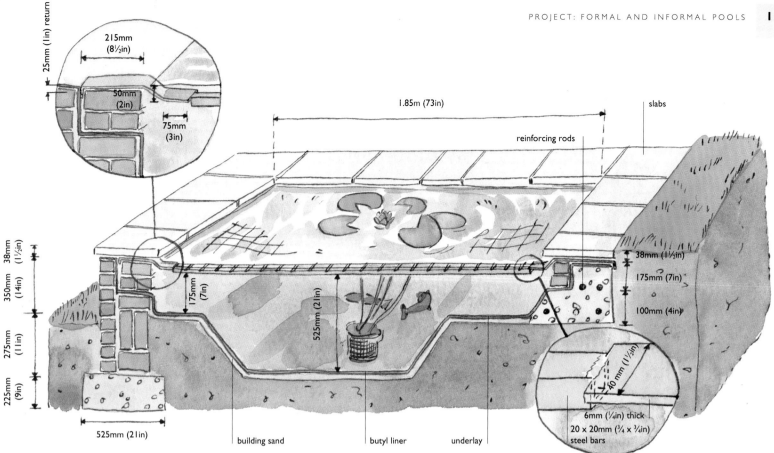

215mm (8½in)

25mm (1in) return

50mm (2in)

75mm (3in)

1.85m (73in)

reinforcing rods

slabs

38mm (1½in)

350mm (14in)

275mm (11in)

225mm (9in)

175mm (7in)

525mm (21in)

525mm (21in)

building sand

butyl liner

underlay

38mm (1½in)

175mm (7in)

100mm (4in)

40 mm (1½in)

6mm (¼in) thick
20 x 20mm (¾ x ¾in)
steel bars

### Constructing the flush coping base

For the flush formal pool surround, excavate about 325mm (13in) below the finished level of the slabs. Lay 100mm (4in) of 1:6 concrete. It is advisable to put reinforcing rods in the concrete where shown. These should be 10mm (³⁄₈in) in diameter.

### Fitting the pool liner

When all the mortar and concrete has set, remove the formwork, put a layer of building sand 25mm (1in) over the base of the pool and trowel up the sides with wet sand. Lay the underlay over the sand, bringing it up over the sides, then folding it into the profile made by the partially completed pool surround. Carefully lay the butyl liner over the underlay, folding it into neat gathers.

### Tucking in the liner for the raised surround

For the raised pool surround, the next stage is to build two courses of 215mm (9in) brickwork (or stone) over the liner, on top of the

blockwork wall. These bricks wedge the liner and hide it if the water level drops.

### Tucking in the liner for the flush surround

For the flush pool surround, lay two courses of 100mm (4in) stretcher bond brickwork over the liner, on top of the concrete. Then bring the liner and underlay up over the back of the brickwork, before laying the next 150mm (6in) depth of 1:6 concrete. This brings the concrete base flush with the top of the brickwork. The top of the concrete and brickwork must be level all around the pool. Lay the underlay and liner on top of the concrete when it has set.

### Positioning the steel straps

The next stage involves positioning the specially made flat steel straps with the box section steel bars welded to them. The steel straps have a 25mm (1in) 'return' to hook over the brickwork of the raised edge or the concrete of the flush edge, with 215 and 390mm

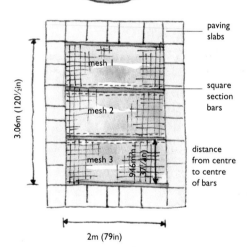

paving slabs

mesh 1

mesh 2

mesh 3

square section bars

distance from centre to centre of bars

3.06m (120½in)

946mm (37¼in)

2m (79in)

(8½ and 15³⁄₈in) horizontal lengths respectively. The bars span the width of the pool finishing about 75mm (3in) from both edges. They are placed at 946mm (37¼in) centres, with the end bars 100mm (4in) from the ends. Before positioning them, put an additional layer of underlay over the liner to cushion the metal strap. Check that the bars are level.

### Fitting the coping

Once the bars have been positioned the coping is mortared on top of the strap and liner, with a generous overhang of about 60m (2½in). Use a 1:4 mix mortar, bedding each slab on three strips of mortar. Use a spirit level to make sure the surround is level. To include an overflow, lay a 25mm (1in) diameter black PVC pipe in the mortar bed, leaving it just proud of the outside edge.

I have never found an overflow necessary, as I prefer to see pools brimming with water. However, in the unlikely event of the pool being brimful of water due to very heavy rain, the grid might be 115mm (4½in) below the water surface, so increasing the risk to very young children. A 22kg (50 pound) child on the middle of the guard would deflect it by an additional 25mm (1in). These conditions are unlikely but, if the safety risk concerns you, install an overflow and check it regularly.

### Installing cables for a pump or lights

If you are installing a submersible pump or light fittings, lay the cables into the pool in the mortar bed under the coping slabs. They should be run through a PVC conduit to prevent them from coming into contact with the mortar. Low-voltage fittings are powered from a transformer in the house. Call in an electrician to install mains voltage versions.

### Preparing the base for planting

When the mortar has set, position underlay over the pool base to cushion the liner, carefully weighing it down with bricks. Again taking care, put a 100–150mm (4–6in) deep layer of soil over the whole base of the pool. Choose a good loam soil, not a fine, silty one which, on being disturbed by fish, creates cloudy water. Now fill the pool, via a double-check valve if using mains water, by resting the end of a hose on the soil in the pool and keeping water pressure to a gentle trickle.

### Planting

First plant the marginal and aquatic plants,

then add the oxygenating plants. If you have constructed the pool in winter, wait until spring to plant all but the oxygenating plants. If you do not like putting top soil in the pool, place the plants in aquatic plant containers, in an appropriate planting compost.

### Positioning the steel grids

Finally, position the grids over the hollow section steel bars. They must be overlapped by at least 100mm (4in). To cover a pool this size, three sheets of 1.22 x 1.85m (48 x 73in) will be necessary. Position the outer two grids 25mm (1in) away from the ends of the pool and centre the other grid over the middle two support bars. Tie them in place with1.6mm thick (16 gauge) galvanized wire, at a maximum of 300mm (12in) centres. Make sure that the ends of the ties are tucked in well.

### MAINTENANCE

Check regularly (at least three times a year) that the structure is safe, making sure that the fixings are secure and that any areas of corroding metal or exposed water are dealt with.

## AN INFORMAL POOL

### THE DESIGN

The illustration shows a cross-section through a typical pool, consisting of the square section metal bars which span 2m (79in) and additional supporting bricks under the liner. The area between the bricks and the edge is filled with soil and marginal plants. In order to make the pool sufficiently natural and irregular, this distance is best varied, making it 600mm (24in) or more in some places and reducing it to half this in others.

### Supporting and positioning the bars

As before, the square section metal bars have flat steel straps welded on to the ends which, this time, have no return and are bolted into concrete through a 10mm (⅜in) diameter hole drilled in both ends. The square section bars for this pool are at 1.02m (40in) centres, with the edge bars not more than 100mm (4in) from the water's edge. The dimensions of the pool shown are about 3.2 x 2m (126 x 79in), but these measurements can be altered provided that you neither increase the 2m (79in)

---

**YOU WILL NEED**
**(for an informal pool)**
- Heavy gauge black butyl liner, 5.7 x 4.2m (18ft 9in x 13ft 9in)
- Underlay, 5.7 x 4.2m (18ft 9in x 13ft 9in), plus additional underlay to cover the liner in planted areas and to create a buffer over bricks, about 5 x 3.8m (16ft 6in x 12ft 6in)
- Eight bricks
- Building sand to protect liner, 0.6 cubic metre, (¾ cubic yard)
- Concrete, 1:6 cement : ballast mix, 0.1 cubic metre (0.13 cubic yard)
- Mortar, 1:5 cement : soft sand mix
- Four 2m (79in) long, 20mm (¾in) square section, galvanized steel bars with a 2.5mm (¹⁄₁₀in) wall thickness, specially made by a blacksmith
- Specially shaped, galvanized steel straps, 40mm (1½in) wide by 6mm (¼in) thick, to be welded to both ends with a hole to take a bolt (see illustration)

- Non-toxic black paint
- Two galvanized steel mesh guards, 1.22 x 2m (48 x 79in), with 3mm (¹⁄₁₆in) bars at 50mm (2in) centres
- One galvanized steel mesh guard, 1.22 x 1.8m (48 x 71in) (Ask a blacksmith to cut the sheets to the required size and smooth off all sharp ends. Paint with a non toxic black paint finish.)
- Eight bolts, 100mm (4in), 10mm (⅜in) in diameter with protective coating
- Eight metal post supports, 600mm (2in) long, to take posts with a base of 75 x 75mm (3 x 3in)
- Galvanized wire for ties, about 1.6mm thick (16 gauge)

**Tools**
- Spade or digger • Shovel • Club hammer • Punch for inserting post supports • Bricklayer's trowel • Wire cutters • Spirit level • String line • Sharp knife or scissors

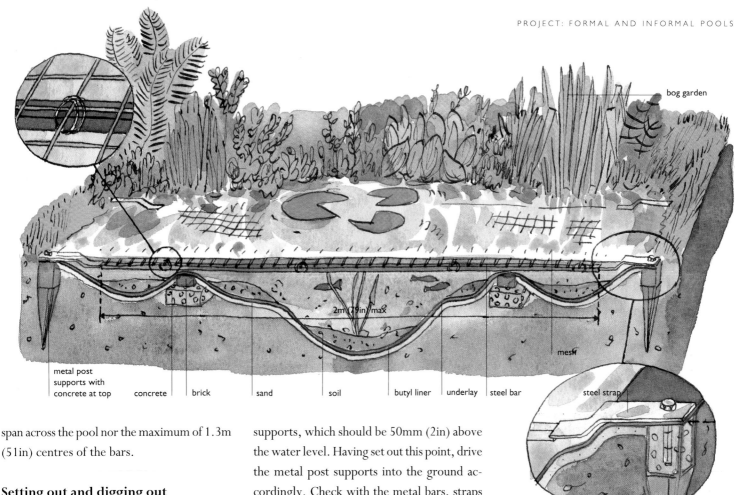

bog garden

2m (79in) max

mesh

metal post
supports with
concrete at top

concrete

brick

sand

soil

butyl liner

underlay

steel bar

steel strap

metal post
support

mesh 1

mesh 2

mesh 3

1.02m
(3ft 4in)

distance
from centre
to centre

bog garden

2m (79in) max.

span across the pool nor the maximum of 1.3m (51in) centres of the bars.

## Setting out and digging out

Having set out the pool and established the proposed water level, dig out the soil to the profiles shown in the illustration. The boundary between the pool and marsh border must be horizontal and 70mm (2¾in) lower than the water level. Set out the positions of the square section bars and dig a hole 400 x 300mm and 175mm deep (16 x 12 x 7in) where each bar crosses the marginal boundary; centre the length of the hole on the bar position. Cast 1:6 mix concrete 100mm (4in) deep in the holes and, when it has set, lay one brick on each concrete pad using 1:5 mix mortar. The bricks must be level 70mm (2¾in) below water level. To provide a smooth base for the liner, add haunching (an angled fillet of mortar) from the top edges of each brick to the edges of its concrete pad.

## Laying the concrete support blocks

Next position the metal post supports around the edge. The holes in the metal straps must be positioned centrally over the metal post

supports, which should be 50mm (2in) above the water level. Having set out this point, drive the metal post supports into the ground accordingly. Check with the metal bars, straps and a level that the positions are correct.

## Preparing the pool for the liner

Follow the same process as for the formal pool. The liner should butt up to the top edge of each post support. Once you have finally adjusted it, lay a double layer of underlay over the concealed bricks to prevent the bars from damaging the liner. Fill the tops of the metal post supports with 1:6 mix concrete, level them off and reposition the straps with the holes over them. Push the 100mm (4in) bolts through the holes and anchor them into the wet concrete.

## Planting

The process is the same as for the formal pool except that the water surface area is reduced. Marginals may be established at the water's edge.

## Positioning the metal grids

Finally, the grids can be positioned over the hollow section steel bars and fixed with metal

ties every 300mm (12in). They must overlap by a minimum of 100mm (4in). To soften the pool edges, either increase the marginal planting or cut the grid appropriately, making sure that no sharp edges are left.

### MAINTENANCE

As for formal pool.

# Simple Water Features

Small, simple water features have a quite different charm to larger pools. They particularly appeal to children, who can identify with the small scale and are fascinated by the movement and magic of the water.

tures a large, water-filled trough with a stone seal perched on the side, squirting water into the container. This is used by the owners' pets – which include dogs, cats and even parrots – as a large drinking bowl.

children are young by building up the base with heaps of pebbles and sand. Even a piece of pipe coming out of a wall may fit the bill, especially if you disguise it by clothing the wall in an abundant climber, such as *Hydrangea petiolaris* or *Clematis armandii*.

### TROUGHS AND SINKS

One of my favourite gardens has a small stone sink on the terrace filled with water, a few aquatic plants, pebbles, some fish, and a few snails. This could hardly be simpler, and the children love it. Another attractive garden fea-

### WALL FEATURES

Masks on walls with water erupting from their mouths into shallow pools are an old favourite and, because detail can be added in so many different ways, rarely become boring. The water level can be kept very shallow while the

### SHALLOW WATER CHANNELS

Shallow channels or runnels of water add an element of fun to a garden. They are ideal for sailing small boats in, and cooling hot, sticky fingers.

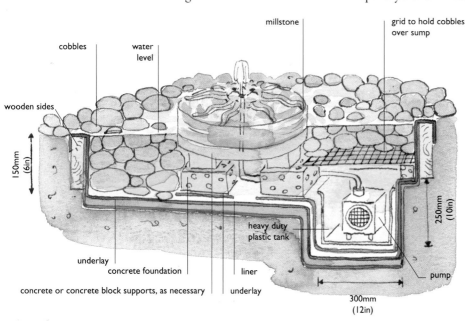

cobbles     water level
wooden sides
millstone          grid to hold cobbles over sump
150mm (6in)
heavy duty plastic tank
250mm (10in)
underlay
concrete foundation     liner
concrete or concrete block supports, as necessary     underlay
pump
300mm (12in)

### How to make bubble fountain
It is possible to buy these in kit form, but they are simple to make yourself.

❶ To install a bubble fountain with an area of damp cobbles around it, first mark out and then excavate the area to a depth of about 150mm (6in). Dig an additional hole for the heavy duty plastic tank which contains a miniature submersible pump, suitable for giving the lift and flow of water required. An electricity supply will be needed for the pump. Ideally, use a low voltage pump powered from a transformer inside the house. Call in an electrician to install the wiring.

❷ Once the concrete or concrete block foundation is laid, place a butyl liner over the underlay and position the tank and pump. Place the millstone on its supports and fit the pipework to connect the fountain and pump. Run the supply lead to the pump through a plastic tube, concealed under the cobbles, to protect it from damage. Place a metal grille over the tank, cover it with cobbles and fill to the brim with water. Top up the water level regularly.

*ABOVE LEFT A delightfully gruesome dragonesque reptile spurts water from its mouth into a long shallow rill. The reptile is made from concrete and was designed and made by Pat Austin.*

*ABOVE CENTRE Water trickles over the perimeter of this scallop-edged bowl into a tiny lower pool. It is a bold yet safe water feature which introduces movement, sound and a suitable environment for water-loving plants, into a small urban garden.*

*ABOVE RIGHT A large clam-shaped dish filled with pretty pebbles and shells will be enjoyed by small children on hot days as well as being kept in use by birds and other wildlife.*

*BELOW LEFT This shallow-water rill is crossed by several little bridges which are attractive to children and contribute to its unique appeal. It was designed by Sir Frederick Gibberd for his own garden.*

*BELOW CENTRE A handsome bubble fountain adds a touch of humour and forms the central focus to a helical theme, it was designed and made by Jessica Slater and is available in different finishes.*

*BELOW RIGHT This small, shallow, brick pool is an ideal expanse of water to arouse young children's interest in aquatic wildlife and plants. Introduce submerged plants and floating aquatics to help to keep algae at bay and to encourage wildlife.*

# The Water's Edge

The edge of a pool is a crucial part of the design. The pool liner should never be revealed – all you should be aware of is the water, the planting and the edging material, if one is used. As water levels will fluctuate, you must ensure that between regular topping-ups the liner does not come into view.

Many materials can be used to edge water, including bricks, granite setts, boulders, slate, marble, exposed aggregate concrete, timber, pebbles, stone or concrete flags, planting or grass. The important thing is to make sure that the construction detail you use is in harmony with the mood of area you are creating.

If you are designing a formal pool using a black butyl liner, it is best to finish the vertical face below the coping which is exposed as the water level drops with an attractive surface such as brick or stone (*see detail on page 111*). This is more complicated to construct than just placing the coping directly over the liner, which, though it can work well, requires you to top up the levels more frequently.

A coping that overhangs by 50–60mm (2–2⅜in) will throw the junction of the lining and coping into heavy shadow, so making it very unobtrusive. If the pool is flush with the ground, bring the liner right back under the coping slab and then vertically up at the back, as this will allow the water level to reach the brim which looks more attractive.

## INFORMAL POOLS

Where a pool has an informal edge it is of equal importance that the black liner does not show. If you are running grass right up to the pool, bring the liner up to form the water's edge at the side of the pool, run it down to a depth of about 20–30cm (8–12in) outside the pool, and then bring it back up again. Fill the pocket thus formed with soil and cut off the liner at ground level, which should be slightly higher than the

*Here a gently sloping area of pebbles at the water side has a wooden decking edge. The shallow slope makes for easy access for frogs, hedgehogs and other animals.*

*Vertical logs contain the edge of the bank. If the pool is made from a flexible liner the fixing should be above it, making the logs mainly cosmetic.*

*Granite setts create an interesting edge detail but must be securely bedded, particularly in a liner pool. The liner should be taken right up behind them.*

*Boulders make a dramatic edge to water provided they look natural. By carrying them on into the water you can increase accessibility.*

*RIGHT This simple bridge leads to a similar area of wooden decking which is adjacent to the water's edge. The edge treatment in the foreground consists of horizontal railway sleepers. The flexible liner comes up the inside edge and is concealed by a horizontal hardwood batten which is screwed to the sleeper.*

water level. Plant the pocket of soil with marginal plants, which will butt up against the mown turf. Soil must cover the liner at the margins, so do not make the slope of the pool too steep or the soil will slide to the bottom of the pool.

In the case of a fairly large informal pool the water's edge is often the most intriguing part, so really exploit it. You may want to run a path around the pool, perhaps placing it hard up to the water's edge at one point then snaking it away through an area of boggy planting, perhaps across some stepping stones or a raised wooden walkway. It could then peter out into a mown area adjacent to the pool, allowing access to the edge again. You could take a boardwalk out over the edge by protecting the liner with some overlay on top of it, and then setting wooden supporting posts in concrete directly on the liner. To give continuity, do not use more than three hard materials.

## POOLSIDE BUILDING

If you have a poolside building in mind, consider putting it on stilts out in the pool so you can sit almost entirely surrounded by water, able to view the wildlife and watch the water rippling in the breeze. The majority of the base of the building can be on solid ground, with a small area cantilevered out over the water partially supported on stilts. Timber decking can also be cantilevered out over the water for a similar feel.

## CREATING A BEACH

Pebbles and boulders, which are now readily available in many garden centres, come into their own when used near water. A gently sloping beach of pebbles can be laid over a butyl liner, creating a natural, attractive edge. Such a beach is excellent for children, as they can wade in gently instead of having to plunge straight to the full depth of the pool, and may

well be a life-saver for small mammals such as hedgehogs which often drown in straight-sided pools. Clumps of marginals can also be used on these pebbly shores, and areas of sand and gravel can be mixed in too. Large boulders can be used as stepping stones, but make sure that a flexible liner is covered with underlay.

## WOODEN EDGING

Railway sleepers are useful for edging an informal pool. The flexible liner can come part or all of the way up the sleeper face edging the water and a hardwood batten can be fixed over the point where the liner ends.

Another method of edging is to use vertical logs. Bring the liner up behind the logs, marginally above water level, and fix the logs over the front. Bearing in mind that the liner should not be punctured, fix the logs at the top, and consider setting the bases in concrete.

# Water Games

Water holds an irresistible allure for children of all ages, and it is not just on hot sunny days that they head for the pool; if it's not warm enough for barefoot paddling they will still enjoy themselves playing pirates, sailing boats or watching the pond life.

The closer to the water they can get the better, so it is worth putting a gently sloping sandy edge in one spot where they can paddle without damaging the liner. A timber structure projecting over the water or a low bridge so that they can sit directly above the water and watch their reflections or drop toys straight in will please them, and stepping stones running over the water are always a firm favourite. A tiny island with restricted access often helps an unnatural water feature to look more natural, provides a refuge for wildlife and stimulates fantasies about castaways.

A source of flowing water will help to increase the oxygen content, so helping to keep the water healthy. It will also provide currents in which to race leaves and toys. Even a shallow rill racing over coloured gravels with recycled water spurting in at one point will prove a big attraction with youngsters.

## POOLS WITHIN POOLS

Younger children can be encouraged to create a series of smaller pools within the main pool by making temporary boundaries with small rocks and pebbles; one could be a fish-free zone for rearing young tadpoles, another could be a haven for newts, and a third a protected pool for baby fish to ensure they do not get swallowed up by large hungry relations. Include some small colourful water plants such as *Mimulus guttatus*, *Myosotis scorpioides* and *Typha minima*, the miniature bullrush.

*LEFT Children and adults appreciate being able to get right down to the water's edge. If you can create shallows for paddling they will undoubtedly be well used. RIGHT This idyllic pastime is not often available in the average domestic garden, but with liner pools on the increase in both number and size, it is now becoming much more achievable.*

*LEFT Pooh sticks is a favourite game which may be played wherever there are bridges and running water. Strategic gaps in the waterside planting here allow access for play. RIGHT Another enjoyable way of using water in the garden is to sail toy boats, whether they be of the sophisticated remote-control type or simple home-made craft.*

# Water Plants

One of the most rewarding tasks in gardening is establishing a water garden, as the plants often grow fast. The best method of establishing aquatic plants is debatable. One system is to containerize all the rooted plants in plastic baskets filled with soil and position them on the floor of the pool; the other is to cover the base of the pool with about 15cm (6in) soil on top of a layer of underlay to protect the liner. This should be a good loam, not a clay soil or one with a fine particle size as these would give a cloudy effect when disturbed by big fish. Unless you have a tiny preformed pool, I would always recommend the latter system as the aquatic plants establish in a more natural-looking way. However, you do have to thin them out annually, or whenever they get too crowded. The other system does give you far greater control of the plants, which can be divided as required.

Algae flourish in bright light, so provide shade to prevent them from thriving. You should aim to have about one third of the surface area of the water in shade, and this can be created by free-floating aquatic plants or the foliage of water lilies and other deep-rooted subjects.

## PLANTING

Carry out the planting in mid- to late spring. Choose a warm day because you will need to get wet! If you have a friend with a well-established pool offer to help thin out the plants, and with luck you might get some pond snails and water boatmen too. If you are using container plants from a garden centre, planting can be done at any time of year.

The oxygenators – submerged rooted plants – such as *Ceratophyllum demersum* (hornwort) and *Potamogeton crispus* (curly pondweed) are vital to a good water balance, which results in clear water without the use of chemicals. Plant them by pushing the ends into the soil and wedging with a rock or brick. I planted *Elodea canadensis* (Canadian pondweed) in mine, and it is extremely vigorous – we pull out about five wheelbarrow-loads twice a year, which the children love doing. We leave the weed on the sides of the pool for about four hours and watch all the wildlife plunge back to the water. However, I think it is best to avoid this one – it is just too prolific!

Plant the other types of rooted plants in a similar way, wedging them down with bricks or stones where necessary. It is much more rough and ready work than putting in a border plant – you do it very fast, partly because your hands start to freeze and also because that is all that is required. The floating plants just need placing – it could not be easier.

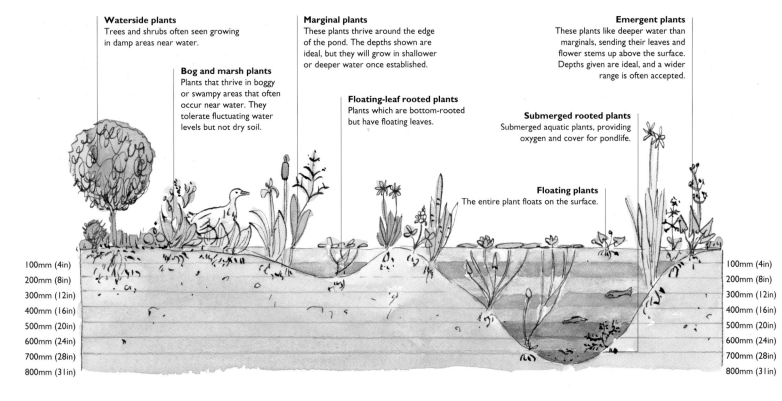

**Waterside plants**
Trees and shrubs often seen growing in damp areas near water.

**Bog and marsh plants**
Plants that thrive in boggy or swampy areas that often occur near water. They tolerate fluctuating water levels but not dry soil.

**Marginal plants**
These plants thrive around the edge of the pond. The depths shown are ideal, but they will grow in shallower or deeper water once established.

**Floating-leaf rooted plants**
Plants which are bottom-rooted but have floating leaves.

**Emergent plants**
These plants like deeper water than marginals, sending their leaves and flower stems up above the surface. Depths given are ideal, and a wider range is often accepted.

**Submerged rooted plants**
Submerged aquatic plants, providing oxygen and cover for pondlife.

**Floating plants**
The entire plant floats on the surface.

100mm (4in)
200mm (8in)
300mm (12in)
400mm (16in)
500mm (20in)
600mm (24in)
700mm (28in)
800mm (31in)

100mm (4in)
200mm (8in)
300mm (12in)
400mm (16in)
500mm (20in)
600mm (24in)
700mm (28in)
800mm (31in)

## Planting positions for water plants

| NAME | DEPTH | COMMENTS |
|---|---|---|
| **Waterside trees and shrubs** | | |
| *Alnus glutinosa* (common alder) | | Establishes and grows very fast; useful on poor subsoils. Height 20m (65ft). **N** |
| *Cornus alba* 'Sibirica' (dogwood) | | Striking red stems, which need cutting back every other year to keep the vibrant colour. Height 3m (10ft). |
| *Salix x chrysocoma* (weeping willow) | | The ideal natural den. Height 12m (40ft). |
| *Salix viminalis* (common osier) | | Use the shoots and young branches to weave a willow den. Height 3m (10ft). **N** |
| *Viburnum opulus* (guelder rose) | | Eye-catching flowers and berries, a most attractive native plant. Height 3m (10ft). **N** |
| **Bog and marsh plants** | | |
| *Gunnera manicata* | | This magnificent large-leaved plant up to 2m (6ft) high adds a tropical feel to damp areas. |
| *Ligularia dentata* 'Desdemona' | | A dramatic plant up to 1.2m (4ft) high with purple-black stems and vivid orange daisy-like flowers. |
| *Petasites japonicus* var. *giganteus* | | This plant can be invasive but is useful for colonizing large areas. Height to 1.5m (5ft). |
| *Primula florindae* | | A stunning plant similar to a giant cowslip which will naturalize in damp zones. Try planting with *P. japonica* 'Millars Crimson'. Height up to 1m (3ft). |
| **Marginal plants** | | |
| *Caltha palustris* (marsh marigold) | 0–15cm (0–6in) | Attractive yellow flowers. **N** |
| *Iris pseudacorus* (yellow flag) | 0–25cm (0–10in) | Vigorous, with eye-catching yellow flowers. **N** |
| *Lysimachia nummularia* (creeping jenny) | 0–5cm (0–2in) | Creeping plant with bright golden flowers. **N** The yellow-leaved form *L. n.* 'Aurea' is more striking. |
| *Lysichiton americanus* (skunk cabbage) | 0–30cm (0–12in) | Bold leaves followed by bright arum-shaped flowers. |
| *Mentha aquatica* (water mint) | 0–20cm (0–8in) | Vigorous plant with lilac flowers and a strong minty aroma. **N** |
| *Mimulus luteus* (monkey musk) | 3–15cm (1¼–6in) | Splendid yellow flowers with maroon and brown spots. |
| *Myosotis scorpioides* (water forget-me-not) | 0–15cm (0–6in) | Has small clusters of bright blue flowers which will flower again if cut back early. **N** |
| *Zantedeschia aethiopica* 'Crowborough' (arum lily) | 0–25cm (0–10in) | A very striking plant with large glossy arrow-shaped leaves and beautiful white flowers. |
| **Emergent plants** | | |
| *Butomus umbellatus* (flowering rush) | 3–25cm (1–10in) | Extremely pretty rosy-pink flowers produced in umbels in early to mid-summer. **N** |
| *Menyanthes trifoliata* (bog bean) | 5–30cm (2–12in) | This spreading plant looks rather like broad beans and has white flowers tipped with pink. **N** |
| *Orontium aquaticum* (golden club) | 25–40cm (10–16in) | Velvety bluish-green leaves, silvery beneath. Curious yellow flowers appear on white stems. |
| *Sagittaria sagittifolia* (arrowhead) | 5–40cm (2–16in) | This plant has arrow-shaped leaves and survives in still and flowing water. **N** |
| *Typha latifolia* (lesser reedmace) | 5–30cm (2–12in) | Smaller relative of *T. angustifolia* (bulrush). Has brown velvety flower spikes; sparrows enjoy the seedheads. **N** |
| **Submerged rooted plants** | | |
| *Callitriche autumnalis* (crystalwort) | 5–60cm (2–24in) | This plant is useful in the autumn and winter as it grows well beneath ice, contributing a fresh, brilliant green, yet can also cope with seasonal drought. **N** |
| *Ceratophyllum demersum* (hornwort) | 30–300cm (1–10ft) | A dark green semi-floating plant with brittle, much-branched stems. **N** |
| *Elodea canadensis* (Canadian pondweed) | 15–200cm (6in–7ft) | A very aggressive plant, so use with care – do not introduce to ponds that will be left untended as it will be too invasive. Excellent for deep water. **N** |
| *Potamogeton crispus* (curly pondweed) | 15–60cm (6–24in) | This plant is at its best in winter and spring when the translucent bronzy-green foliage is evident, before disintegrating in mid-summer. |
| **Floating-leaf rooted plants** | | |
| *Nymphaea alba* (white waterlily) | 30cm–3m (1–10ft) | Blooms 10–15cm (4–6in) across, probably too big for most ponds, but wonderful where space allows. **N** |
| *Nuphar lutea* (common pond lily) | 50cm–3m (20in–10ft) | A vigorous plant that will tolerate running water and heavy shade. It has bright yellow flowers 4–5cm (1½–2in) across with a strong alcoholic smell. Rather rampant so not ideal for garden ponds. **N** |
| *Nymphoides peltata* (fringed waterlily) | 10–75cm (4–30in) | Small, bright green leaves and clear yellow-fringed flowers. Suitable for smaller ponds. |
| *Ranunculus aquatilis* (water crowfoot) | 10–60cm (4–24in) | Attractive, buttercup-like white flowers with yellow centres appear in spring. |
| **Floating plants** | | |
| *Azolla filiculoides* (fairy moss, water fern) | | This attractive fern changes colour from pale green to rusty red in late summer in full sun. Do not let it cover all the pool as it will prevent oxygen from reaching the water. **N** |
| *Eichhornia crassipes* 'Major' (floating water hyacinth) | | Beautiful hyacinth-like flowers. Remove to frost-free quarters in autumn. |
| *Lemma minor* (duckweed) | | Many will pay to get this plant removed, but in certain places it looks the part. **N** |
| *Stratiotes aloides* (floating water soldier) | | This fascinating plant resembles the cut-off top of a pineapple. The foliage in young plants is a reddish-bronze colour. **N** |

**N** = native or commonly naturalized

# Water Maintenance

When you are establishing a pond the ideal is to create a healthy natural balance which to a certain extent will regulate itself. However, most garden ponds are not natural. They have no constant supply of water such as an organic pond would have and you will have to top yours up from time to time, probably with water from a treated source. This is likely to be relatively rich in nutrients and may tip the balance of your pool, causing the algae to proliferate. The best way therefore, is to top it up frequently, so that you do not put large quantities in at one go.

## CONTROLLING THE VEGETATION

Aquatic plants are often astonishingly robust and will need tackling about once a year to bring them back in line, otherwise they will eventually cover any water less than 1.8m (6ft) deep. Oxygenators, particularly ones such as *Elodea canadensis* (Canadian pondweed) and *Myriophyllum spicatum* (spiked water milfoil), will need thinning out once or even twice a year. In spring, any marginal and emergent plants that are becoming overwhelming will also need to be divided, thinned or cleared.

In spring and/or autumn dead stems and leaves of plants can be cut down and removed, and the growth tidied up. If you have fish in the pool this is better done in autumn as stems and dying leaves will rot down, causing a higher concentration of decomposing matter and thus undesirable gases in the water. If there are many trees nearby, you should remove excessive fallen leaves from the bottom of the pool or net it for a while to catch the leaves.

Once the pool has become established you may find an algal bloom of blanket weed occurs. A simple way of combating this and many other forms of algae is to sink some barley straw which, when it rots, releases algal inhibitors (other types of straw are not so effective).

## WINTER MAINTENANCE

During winter place a soft rubber ball in a straight-sided pool to prevent the expanding

*This green slime is blanket weed, which sometimes occurs during the warmer months. It is a natural response to extra fertility, but if it takes over it can reduce the available oxygen.*

action of ice cracking the sides. If you have fish, do not let the water freeze over for more than a week as this could harm them. Install a heater, cover a small section to stop it freezing or melt the ice with warm bottles. Do not use a hammer to crack ice as shock waves will damage pondlife.

There should be no need to empty the pond out and clean it, and indeed this would be detrimental to the wildlife. However, you may find that the amount of sediment at the bottom builds up, in which case try removing a few buckets of mud in early autumn before the water creatures have begun to hibernate.

Consult your pump supplier to see what treatment is recommended during the winter with respect to draining the system. In the case of submersible pumps the advice is usually to run them every other week for just a few minutes to keep them ticking over.

*In this small pool the plants are in containers, limiting the vigorous varieties which would otherwise colonize the entire pool. In larger pools a more natural effect is gained by planting directly into soil on the pool base.*

## Water Problems and Solutions

| PROBLEM | SOLUTION |
| --- | --- |
| Loss of water through evaporation | Top up the water level regularly. If using chlorinated water, never add more than a quarter of the total volume at a time. |
| Loss of water through leaks | Most liners can be repaired. Drain the water to the level of the leak (removing fish, etc. if necessary), find the leak and patch up. |
| Cloudy water, usually caused by<br>  i) not enough oxygenating plants<br>  ii) too much sunlight on water<br>  iii) Disturbance of very fine silty or clay soils on bottom by large fish<br>  iv) Water balance has not yet had time to establish | <br>i) Add more oxygenating plants.<br>ii) Put in additional plants such as water lilies to create shade.<br>iii) Remove silt or stabilize it by adding a gravel layer on top.<br><br>iv) Be patient, allow time to let the natural balance establish – this may take a growing season. |
| Loss of fish to predators such as herons, gulls, kingfishers and cats | Add plants with large floating leaves such as water lilies for cover and/or place a trip wire about 45cm (18in) high around the pond to deter birds such as herons that fish from the water's edge. |
| Fish gasping for oxygen in hot summers | Give short-term relief by letting water sprinkle over pool surface. For a long-term solution, add more oxygenating plants, or some water circulation device such as a pump and fountain. |
| Ice over pool | In winter the expanding action of ice can cause straight-sided pools to crack, so float a soft ball on the surface to relieve the pressure. If there are fish in the pool and the water surface is frozen for a week or more, make one or two holes to allow toxic gases to escape. Do not smash the ice, as this will damage fish and amphibians; instead, place a plastic bottle filled with hot water on the ice, refilling as necessary. Alternatively, place a purpose-built heater in the water, or cover a small area with some insulation. |
| Fish dying in cold weather | This may be caused by feeding when the water temperature is below 15°C (60°F), in which case the food will decompose in the fish before their metabolism (which slows down in winter) can break it down. Do not feed fish unless water is above this temperature. |
| Overcrowded and overgrown aquatic plants | Partially clear areas of plants where they are becoming too invasive. Leave discarded plants by the pool for long enough to allow pondlife to crawl back to the water. Divide water lilies up when leaves start standing proud of the water and replant giving a good feed of water lily pellets or balls of bonemeal mixed with soil, buried in the compost. |
| Blanket weed (*Cladophora*) over surface of pool | Sink some barley straw which will release algae inhibitors and also increase the invertebrate population, some of which will feed on the algae. Put some barley straw in an old onion bag or other netting. It is important that the straw is well aerated, which is to say not too tightly packed together – the recommended rate is 50g per m³ (1½oz per cu yd). Anchor it just below the surface or near an inflow or fountain. After one to four months your blanket weed problem should disappear. This is best carried out in the spring, before significant problems with algae have had a chance to build up and become entrenched in your pool. |

# A Garden For Wildlife and Pets

*The pleasure that children derive from animals is enhanced by a more relaxed approach to gardening; just mowing the lawn a little higher, leaving seedheads on plants through the winter and keeping some of your dead logs and debris instead of tidying everything away will immediately make the garden more desirable to wildlife. Pet-lovers will also appreciate well-designed pet hutches which house the animal handsomely without detracting from the garden's beauty.*

# The Wildlife Garden

The more the world around us becomes covered with concrete and brick, the more our appreciation of natural habitats such as woodland, meadows and water tends to increase. To be able to hear birds singing, smell a freshly cut flowering meadow and observe frogs hunting for slugs is a refreshing change from noisy lorries, choking exhausts and sterile surfaces. To this end, many gardeners are adapting their plots to make them more sympathetic towards the needs of wildlife.

## PROVIDING HABITATS

A wildlife garden does not have to be a form-less wilderness – it can be designed to cater for the family's needs just like any garden, with colourful plants, plenty of contrast and areas for relaxing and *al fresco* eating. The main difference is that to encourage wildlife you aim to provide a range of habitats, and when it comes to maintenance you give the require-ments of wildlife preference over a tidy appearance. This may involve, for example, leaving dead flowerheads on many plants such as *Helianthus* (sunflower), *Lunaria* (honesty) and *Echinops* (globe thistle) so that birds and insects can feed on them through the winter months. Instead of cutting your herbaceous plants to the ground at the end of the growing season, you leave most of them intact to allow a multitude of insects to inhabit exposed hollow stems. You may have a pile or two of dead logs in a quiet place safe from distur-bance, an ideal habitat for various fungi, amphibians such as young newts and many in-sects including wood wasps, spiders and beetle grubs, which in turn will attract hedgehogs, thrushes, wrens and blackbirds.

## CHOOSING PLANTS

Another difference between a wildlife garden and a more conventional garden is the range

*By attracting insects into your garden you will in turn encourage the birds and mammals which feed on them. Few insects are as spectacular as some butterflies, but all play their part in a rich wildlife garden.*

of plants you choose to grow; ideally you should plant 60–70 per cent native species. If you find the lack of horticultural variety dis-maying go ahead and grow what interests you, but remember that native species will support a far greater number and variety of wildlife than exotic species – for instance, gall wasps live on *Rosa canina*, the native rose, but are unable to survive on cultivated roses. Very few insects live on plane trees as the leaves are not palatable, but hundreds of different insects, birds and mammals can live on an oak tree, so if you have space for only one large tree, make sure it is one that wildlife will like. Native plants will generally be a host to all sorts of mildews, insects and viruses and will tolerate them quite happily and unobtrusively, whereas a cultivated plant may require a spray that will

*On a warm day this area of long grass studded with wild flowers is alive with the sounds of many insects, birds and small mammals. It requires much less maintenance than a traditional lawn.*

slaughter every insect around. Although you may not find insects the most glamorous of visitors to your garden, they are a vital part of the food chain, providing food for many birds and small mammals. You will be more likely to attract the more lovable forms of wildlife if you have a varied and prolific range of them.

Even in a small urban garden you will be able to re-create many wildlife habitats such as woodland, wildflower meadows, pool and wetland, designed to be just as charming as a conventional garden. A woodland edge sur-rounding the garden can be planted to provide privacy and shelter, and may contain a good mix of shrubs and a few native trees underplanted with bluebells, primroses and foxgloves. A mown path could meander through a flowering meadow bordering a marshy area which surrounds a large, natural-looking pool.

The conventional garden tends to rely heav-ily on evergreens to add colour and interest in the winter months. A wildlife garden has a smaller proportion of evergreens and other factors such as berries and seedpods take prec-edence, looking particularly stunning on a frosty morning. In order to provide extra in-terest you may want to add other elements

*Foxgloves provide a wonderful woodland edge effect and are one of the simplest plants to grow from seed. They are biennial, so make sure that the seedlings are not inadvertently weeded out. They have a charming trait of coming up in places where it would be impossible to plant them, such as tiny cracks at the base of outdoor buildings.*

*Although grey squirrels are fun to watch they are a mixed blessing as they can do damage to young trees, feasting on the tender green shoots. They will also steal food from bird tables.*

such as an attractive garden building which could be used as an observation hide as well as a focal point, a boardwalk over your marsh, an eye-catching gate, a pergola to create a shaded walk and interesting fencing or walls. These features do not have to be rustic in de-sign or finish – they are an opportunity to bring in some striking tints and shades such as slaty blues, grey-greens, rusts or terracottas which will contribute colour on a dull winter day.

### CONSTRUCTION FOR WILDLIFE

Bear wildlife in mind when you are doing any work in the garden. If you build a dry-stone wall, leave larger than normal gaps at the base for toads; try to lay your paving on sand rather than concrete so insects can live under your paving stones; provide a generous bird-feeding area out of the way of the local cats;

position bird boxes with a range of hole sizes liberally around your garden; put up a bat box or two; make some good compost heaps which provide a suitable home for slow worms and grass snakes; raise the height of your lawnmower blades about 25mm (1in) and your lawn will be far more attractive for in-sects and the grass will become increasingly invaded by wild flowers. Try to reduce the amount of weedkillers, insecticides and fungi-cides you use treating them as a last resort.

A useful analogy put forward by Chris Baines, founder of the Urban Wildlife Group, is to compare your garden with a service station. Wildlife will visit you to refuel. If you make a really excellent service station that provides a good range of sustenance, you will have visitors from far and wide dropping in on a regular basis.

# Attracting Wildlife

### BIRDS

Many of our favourite garden birds nest in hollow tree trunks or holes in rotten branches, but gardeners tend to remove these in the interests of safety. Nesting boxes make a good alternative – camouflage them well, put them out of direct sun, and provide several with different-sized holes from 30mm (1⅛in) to 50mm (2in) in diameter. Put up a bird table which provides food at different levels for different types of feeders: on the table, hanging below it and on the ground beneath. Do not site the table where there is plenty of camouflage for a stalking cat. A pool or constant water source, especially in icy weather, is vital for birds, which need to bathe as well as drink.

### FOXES

Urban foxes are on the increase, attracted by the varied food supplies in our dustbins. They are predominantly nocturnal, so be on the look-out at dusk for a glimpse of a fox scavenging for a food source such as a plump domestic rabbit. You will know if you have a resident fox from the overpowering and distinctive smell which they use to mark their territory. Putting out pet food at the same time each day will encourage them to return. Occasionally, they occupy the area beneath garden sheds for their daytime hideaway, and they also like dense shrubbery.

### LADYBIRDS

There are few insects which are looked on as favourably as the ladybird. Apart from their pretty spotted appearance, of which there are many different versions (there are some 45 species in England), they are useful to have in your garden as both the adult and the immature larvae will eat through vast quantities of greenfly, blackfly and other pests. To encourage them, make an insect hibernator (*see right*) by fixing a panel of hollow stems of various sizes, taken from herbaceous plants, to a wall.

## HEDGEHOGS

Hedgehogs enjoy a diet rich in slugs, snails and insects, so a heap of decaying wood provides a good hedgehog diner. Make a simple hibernator by building a pile of branches and leaves in a quiet location, leaving a small gap for access. Never set fire to heaps of vegetation in autumn and winter without checking for the presence of hibernating hedgehogs (and do not build a Guy Fawkes or Halloween bonfire in advance). Do not use slug pellets as they may kill hedgehogs too. If you have a fence all around your garden leave a few small gaps for hedgehogs to come and go, and if you are using nylon garden netting over vegetables raise it at least 10–15cm (4–6 in) above the ground otherwise they may become caught in it; you can surround the netting with solid wood or plastic edging to keep birds out. Lastly, *never* leave out bread and milk – while hedgehogs will tuck into it with enthusiasm, milk upsets their digestion and encourages infection. If you feel their natural diet is in short supply, tinned dog food is the best alternative.

## DUCKS

If you have a quiet pool in your garden you might find that wild ducks will come winging in to make use of it. In Holland, nesting baskets on stilts have been used for centuries with great success. These are predator-proof, provided they are sited away from overhanging branches which a rat might make its way along. The lowest part of the basket should be about 20cm (8in) above the water. Unless the ducks are familiar with an aerial nest site such as this, they may take time to discover its purpose.

## BATS

The rather spooky image of bats is gained mainly from the blood-sucking activity of the vampire bat, which is indigenous to Central and South America and far removed in all senses from our insect-eating native species of bat. Several of these are threatened with extinction, so count yourself lucky if you can watch bats hunting for food on a calm summer evening; growing night-scented flowers and leaving an outside light on at dusk will attract moths and other night-flying insects that form a major food source. Bats' main roosting sites have been in roof cavities and old barns, but the availability of these has diminished dramatically as a result of the toxic chemicals used for treating wood and the conversion of barns to housing. You can attract these delightful creatures by putting up a bat box on a shel-tered, quiet wall or tree, training climbers against battens fixed to a wall or fence or by building a dry-stone wall 'rockery' with cavities that will house their prey as well as the bats themselves.

# A Wildlife Garden Plan

THIS IS VERY MUCH A FAMILY GARDEN, DESIGNED TO INCLUDE THE REQUIREMENTS OF THREE GREGARIOUS
TEENAGERS AGED BETWEEN TEN AND SIXTEEN.

A wide terrace next to the modern house is continually used for eating and entertaining, and
has large glazed doors and windows which look over the water to the garden house. From
here a bird feeding station can also be observed.

### THE GARDEN HOUSE

The walls are made from woven willow branches with layers of wet loam combined with straw
thrown against the willow frame. The sun baked the walls hard and a lime wash was then applied inside and out, purely for aesthetic purposes. The mud walls would not stand up to
continuous rain, so the roof has a generous overhang. There are bat and bird boxes built into the
house, and the floor is wooden rather than concrete in the hope that a fox might make an earth
beneath it. A short stretch of curving stone wall leading from the house has larger holes at the
bottom which form tempting dank refuges for toads.

### THE WATER

The water has marshy areas around it which seethe with wildlife. To give more timid occupants
shelter, the area between the pool and fence has only limited accessibility. A boardwalk projecting over the water is frequently used by the children. This area is very visible from the house,
and as such is easy for the parents to monitor and provides a continual source of interest.

### THE WOODLAND AREA

A mown grass path meanders from the much-used large paved area past the pool on to a tiny
'woodland' area. In a small glade a circular turf bank contains a large sandpit, where the children come to read, play games or chat. The area under the trees has longer grass studded with
wild flowers. The trees support hammocks, ropes, swings and platforms and shelter small en-
campments. Over the years the children have altered this area according to whim. Its contribution
to the wildlife in the garden has been of equal importance, as it has provided nectar, seeds,
fruits, foliage and accommodation for insects, mammals and amphibians.

### THE VEGETABLE GARDEN

The vegetable garden is separated by a willow fence, covered in summer with runner beans, climbing nasturtiums and sweet peas. A willow
tepee provides an organic Wendy house, and the mushroom garden
sited next to it provides as much fascination as food. The stones and
boulders are really there to provide a home for lizards and insects, but
are repeatedly disturbed by the children using them as building materials for some new project or other. A pile of decaying wood is home to
myriad insects, amphibians and fungi.

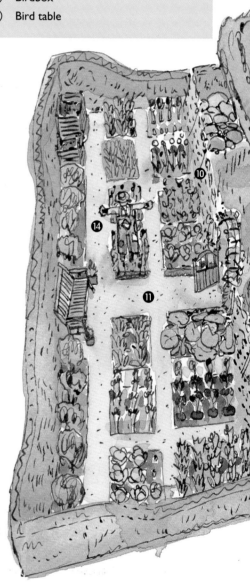

## THE PLAN

| | | |
|---|---|---|
| ① | Wildlife pool | ⑩ Willow hedge |
| ② | Garden house | ⑪ Vegetable garden |
| ③ | Herb garden | ⑫ Insect hibernator |
| ④ | Stone wall | ⑬ Pegged tree with |
| ⑤ | Turf bunk and | slide |
| | sandpit | ⑭ Scarecrow |
| ⑥ | Mushroom | ⑮ Swing |
| | garden | |
| ⑦ | Willow wigwam | |
| ⑧ | Birdbox | |
| ⑨ | Bird table | |

*Even in a wildlife garden you may want to direct the
birds away from your vegetables, and using a scarecrow
is a charmingly traditional and colourful way to do it.*

The garden building has a simple timber frame with willow branches woven around it. This was then clad with a mixture of a mud loam combined with straw. It is important to make walls like this during a long hot spell so that they bake hard. A white limewash has been applied, but external paint of any colour could be used. The roof must have a generous overhang to provide protection from the rain.

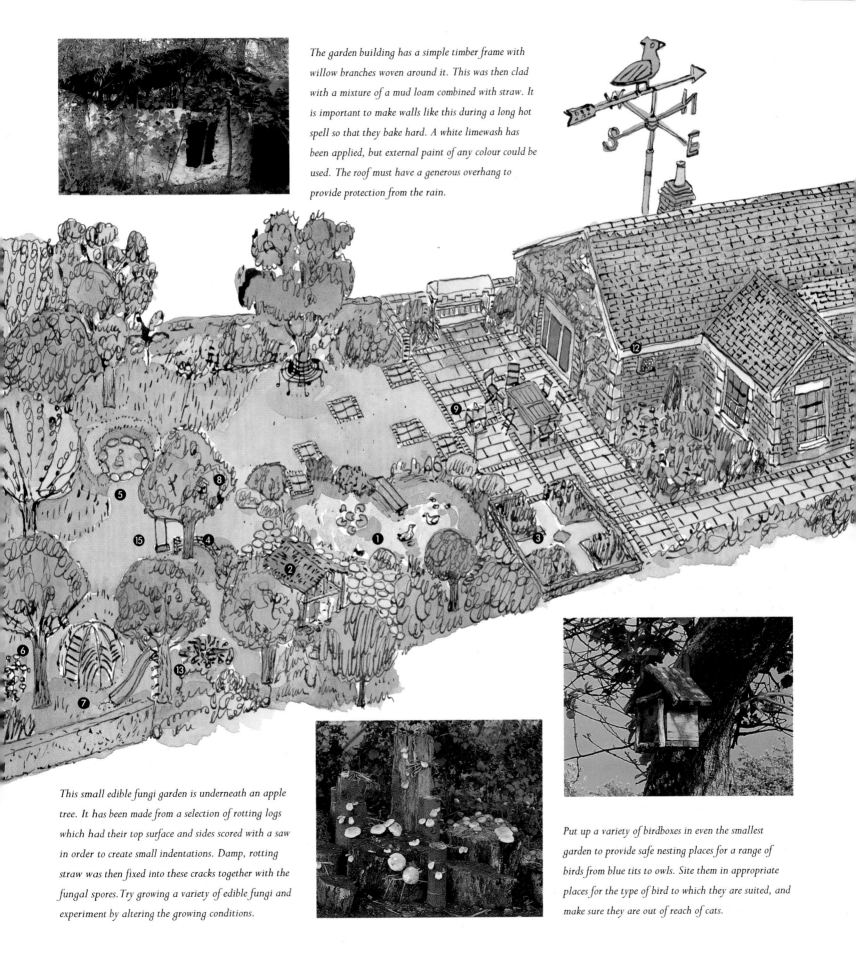

This small edible fungi garden is underneath an apple tree. It has been made from a selection of rotting logs which had their top surface and sides scored with a saw in order to create small indentations. Damp, rotting straw was then fixed into these cracks together with the fungal spores. Try growing a variety of edible fungi and experiment by altering the growing conditions.

Put up a variety of birdboxes in even the smallest garden to provide safe nesting places for a range of birds from blue tits to owls. Site them in appropriate places for the type of bird to which they are suited, and make sure they are out of reach of cats.

# The Wildflower Meadow

Ninety-five per cent of English wildflower meadows have been destroyed over the past 25 years. Even the specially designated areas that are particularly valuable in terms of flora or fauna, the Sites of Special Scientific Interest (SSSI), are disappearing at a rate of 10 per cent a year. Although you may think that growing a few square metres of wild flowers is not going to solve the problem, the area of small gardens in England adds up to something over a million acres so your contribution would be by no means insignificant.

Another reason for growing wild flowers amid long grass is that it is a relaxing form of gardening which can take as much or as little time as you wish; the basic requirement is only one or possibly two cuts a year. If you are tidy-minded you will have to take a firm hold of yourself during July, once the main show of flowers is over, and wait for your tousled meadow to set seed. Only then can you get out the scythe, rotary mower or shears, otherwise you will be disappointed by a meagre show the following year. Wide bands mown around the area and paths mown through it do make it look more respectable, although in time you may well become happily attuned to a less kempt garden.

If you are going to manage the meadow particularly for the benefit of insects, bear in mind that above all they require a variety of habitats. An ideal grassland will provide a mix of short open turf, tall grass, tussocks, scrub and patches of bare sunbaked ground.

### CHOOSING FLOWERS

The ideal soil for wild flowers is a poor topsoil. If your garden is blessed with a good thick loam, remove it to where it will be better ap-

LEFT *A wildflower meadow in the garden provides a wonderfully natural-looking area and is a superb habitat for many insects and small mammals. It is a convenient way to treat small or large areas of grass, requiring only basic maintenance levels if that is all you have time for.*

preciated. If this is not feasible, plant species which can compete with the more vigorous grasses, such as *Centaurea* spp. (knapweeds), *Malva moschata* (musk mallow), *Knautia arvensis* (field scabious), *Silene vulgaris* (bladder campion) and *Tanacetum vulgare* (tansy).

You may want several different patches of flowering meadow to broaden the attraction for wildlife. This can be achieved by planting spring bulbs and early-flowering plants such as *Ajuga reptans* (bugle), *Primula veris* (cowslip), *Bellis perennis* (daisy), *Cardamine pratensis* (lady's smock) and *Hypochoeris radicata* (cat's

ear). These will have finished flowering and set seed by early to mid-summer and can be mown then. A late-flowering meadow with *Malva moschata* (musk mallow), *Salvia pratensis* (meadow clary), *Centaurea nigra* (hardhead), *Centaurea cyanus* (cornflower) and *Knautia arvensis* (field scabious) can be mown until early summer and again in early to mid-autumn.

### CULTIVATION

Many wildflower seed firms produce informative brochures to guide your choice. Nevertheless, many people report a poor success rate when they try to establish wild flowers from seed. This is probably because it is often not realized that perennial wild flowers tend not to flower in the first season after germinating. Also, some of the flowering annuals are best suited to growing on regularly disturbed land and will fade out quickly unless they are resown or the ground turned, and some seeds only germinate if they are very fresh or have had several winters' worth of cold weather.

### SOWING SEED

If you do decide to use seed, your success rate will increase if you sow the seeds into seed trays of potting compost in the late summer and plant them on into small plant pots when they have three or four leaves. Plant them out in their final position in the following autumn, some 12 months later, and water until established.

If you are starting your meadow from scratch, let all the weeds present germinate and then remove them with a hoe or a non-selective, non-residual, systemic weed-killer such as glyphosate. Next sow the grass seed in late summer at about 20g per m$^2$ (½oz per sq yd), or about a fifth of the usual rate. As long as it does not contain any rye grass (which would swamp most of the flowers) do not

worry which grass mixture you use as the end product will probably be the same. Then oversow this with a wildflower mixture of your choice: for example, a simple mix of *Chrysanthemum leucanthemum* (oxeye daisy) and *Rhianthus minor* (yellow rattle).

Rake the seed over and firm the seedbed by treading or light rolling. Water if conditions are dry, but be careful not to wash all the seed out. More precious plants can be planted in small plugs the next autumn when the meadow has established.

*LEFT Mown paths and edges allow you within easy reach of the various flowering herbs and grasses and also form neater edges to these less structured parts of the garden. This is particularly useful when the flowering meadow goes to seed in summer and looks rather unkempt.*

## From lawn to wildflower meadow

### Autumn
❶ Reduce soil fertility by removing patches of turf and topsoil about 30 x 30cm (12 x 12in) and replacing with weed-free subsoil.
❷ Put in the plants (not seeds), either purchased growing in plugs or home-propagated, keeping to one type of plant in each patch. Include *Chrysanthemum leucanthemum* (oxeye daisy), which is an easy starter. Water the plants in until they become established. Planting may also be done in early spring.

❸ Put in the spring-flowering bulbs, such as *Narcissus pseudo-narcissus* (native daffodil), *Fritillaria meleagris* (snake's head fritillary), *Scilla nutans* (English bluebell), *Tulipa sylvestris* (wild tulip), *Galanthus nivalis* (snowdrop) and *Ornithogalum umbellatum* (star of Bethlehem), depending on conditions.

### Spring
Remove any pernicious plants such as nettles, dock or creeping thistle by hand. Carry on doing this throughout the growing season. (If your meadow has a high proportion of these and/or coarse grasses at the outset, remove

them by tight mowing for a year prior to introducing the wild flowers.)

### Mid- to late summer
When the flowers have set seed, cut the grass to about 75mm (3in). Leave the 'hay' for a week or two so the seeds drop into the meadow, then remove it to maintain a low soil fertility.

### Mid- to late autumn
Carry out the final cut, removing the cuttings before the spring bulbs start pushing through the turf. This cut ensures that they do not have too much competition.

# The Wetland Habitat

Wetland habitats are disappearing every day as ponds are filled in and marshy areas drained to create more productive agricultural land, while what wetland remains is polluted with agrochemicals. Wildlife such as frogs and newts were becoming rare until recently, when garden pools became popular with the advent of easy-to-use modern liners.

Creating a wildlife pool with a surrounding area of wetland is one of the most enthralling tasks in gardening, and as soon as it is finished all sorts of wildlife will start to colonize it. To enjoy your water to the full, site it where it can be observed from the house, allowing the sunlight to fall on it from the south at least, and try to make one side fairly inaccessible to people so that the shyer animals can be left alone. Ideally there should not be too many overhanging trees, as the rotting leaves will affect the chemical balance of the water. The site should be level as other-

wise you will have to bank one or both edges, which will present you with problems in trying to make it look natural. Try to make the pool in proportion to the site, opting for a generous size if you can. A pool smaller than about 2 x 1.2m (6½ x 4ft) is going to mean hard work before a good balance is established; it will be difficult to achieve clear water without using chemicals.

## CREATING A POOL

Although it may seem like a good idea to make a pool in an existing damp spot, it is awkward digging in wet sludge. Unless you are going to line it with puddled clay a liner pool in a dryer spot is an easier job. Puddled clay has gone out of fashion now, but if you have a local supply of good blue clay to hand, consider using it. You need to make sure that the base is below the water table so that the clay is kept moist in dry periods, otherwise it will dry out

and crack, releasing the water. Line the sides of the pool with clay to a depth of about 15cm (6in) and compact it well so it smears. Put soil on top for planting.

For a liner pool, use a heavy gauge butyl rubber, or black polythene of at least 1000 gauge. Protect the liner from the underside with newspapers, underlay, old carpet or sand, and also protect the top in areas where you are going to plant with more underlay under the planting medium. The sun will degrade the lining, so make sure that it is not exposed.

When you dig your pool, ensure that the sides slope very gently in places to create shallow edges, and make the depth at least 60cm (2ft) in order to prevent the pool freezing completely in cold winters.

After filling the pool, you can start to plant it up in the spring. In that first season, as the plants and aquatic animals start to colonize the water, you will find that it quickly turns a

*LEFT As a result of the reduction of wetland areas many British species of dragonfly have become extinct in the last 50 years. Dragonflies feast on midges and other tiny insects that live in damp areas and among meadow grasses and flowers. Keep your eyes peeled when you are in the vicinity of your pool and you will observe dragonflies mating, hunting and laying their eggs.*

*ABOVE Frogs have benefited immensely from the boom in artificial garden pools and they are now widespread in gardens. They are attractive and also* *useful, as they eat slugs. If you want to maximize their numbers you should not stock your pool with fish as they will eat the tadpoles.*

LEFT *This small marshy area and pool provide a little wetland area which is mainly tended by two young children. Frogs, toads, newts, dragonflies, water snails and other varieties of wildlife arrived very soon after it was constructed. It is situated a stone's throw from the kitchen window so that it is under almost constant observation from the house.*

startling spinach green and given good weather may well maintain this lurid colour all summer. Do not be tempted by bottles of chemicals and electronic filters, but watch the natural balance start to take over and gradually clear the water; in some cases only a month will pass before the algal bloom is cleared up as long as you have adequate oxygenating plants – one plant per 30cm$^2$ (5sq in) of surface water is recommended, preferably of several different varieties. Make sure you include some water snails. Garden centres sell grey water fleas (*Daphnia*), which eat algae and so help to clear the water.

When choosing your aquatic plants it is no hardship to select predominantly native ones, as there are plenty with interesting foliage and/or charming flowers. They are also generally easier to establish. Two of my favourite waterside plants which seem particularly attractive to wildlife are *Eupatorium cannabinum* (hemp agrimony) and *Ajuga reptans* (bugle),

loved by butterflies and bees respectively. Both like damp spots, so if you have a liner pool on free-draining soil you will have to create a boggy area beside it. This is in any case worth doing as it widens your horticultural scope considerably.

## CREATING A BOGGY AREA

To make a boggy area, dig out the area required (a minimum of 1–2m$^2$/11–22sq ft) to a minimum depth of 30cm (12in) or a good 60cm (2ft) if you want to include some of the larger exotic plants, and line it with heavy-gauge polythene. Puncture a few small holes in it and fill it up with a good loam.

I would include some exotic plants in this area, though true wildlife gardeners would take a more purist attitude. Some of my favourites are the candelabra primulas, such as *Primula florindae* with its pale yellow flowers and *P. japonica* 'Miller's Crimson', a vivid pink that looks stunning in wide mixed drifts. The

ornamental rhubarb *Rheum palmatum* makes a great statement and is easy to grow. If you want to stick to natives you can enjoy the more subtle charms of *Lysimachia nummularia* (creeping Jenny) and *Lychnis flos-cuculi* (ragged robin), to name two of my favourites.

## INTRODUCING FISH

To many gardeners one of the attractions of a pool is to watch the fish, and the common goldfish is cheap and easy. The drawback is that they will eat vast quantities of frogspawn and tadpoles, so for a true wildlife pool you should really leave them out and settle for a few stickleback, provided the pool is large enough, and maybe one or two tench to help eat some of the debris in the bottom.

When you top up the pool, which will be especially necessary in summer, take care not to replace more than a quarter of the water with chlorinated water as too much of this will affect the balance and encourage algae.

# Woodland and Coppice

A patch of woodland, even if it is only a strip some 3m (10ft) wide, introduces a mysterious shady quality into part of your garden. It also enables you to provide a multi-tiered woodland edge bringing in a versatile range of habitats for plants and animals. Do not be put off by the expense or the need for patience – the most successful type of tree planting uses two- to three-year-old transplants (not costly standards) and it is worth waiting for five years or so to reap such rich rewards.

Dense tree and shrub planting has many other benefits, too. It provides shelter, useful in any garden as it enables you to enjoy it on a far more regular basis and hastens the growth of all the plants by creating a warmer, kinder micro-climate; it screens out eyesores and diverts the attention to attractive elements (even a superb view is often improved by defining it with planting); and for children it provides a tough environment where they can climb, swing and hide, as well as concealing items such as climbing frames and swings.

## PLANTING FOR QUICK RESULTS

You will probably want to encourage a wide range of invertebrates, birds, mammals both large and small and amphibians, so you will need to provide rich habitats at various different levels, trying to keep to predominantly native species. If you are starting from scratch and lack patience, the use of a 'nurse' crop of quick-growing species is essential. *Betula pendula* (birch), *Alnus glutinosa* (alder), *Prunus avium* (wild cherry) and *Acer campestre* (field maple) will tolerate exposed windy sites, grow fast and so provide a more sheltered environment for the slower-growing species, such as oak, beech or ash, which will eventually form the backbone of your wood or coppice. If you do not have enough space to accommodate such large trees, go for a closely planted group of smaller native trees such as *Ilex aquifolium* (holly), *Sorbus aucuparia* (mountain ash), *Corylus avellana* (hazel) or *Prunus padus* (bird cherry) which will still give that evocative woodland character.

One of the most important factors in getting trees to establish fast is to choose the right tree for the soil. I have found that on our very

*BELOW In this small woodland area, trees are planted at a minimum of 1.5m (5ft) centres for quick results. This area is about 10m (32ft) wide by 5m (16½ft) long. The section line AA is shown in detail overleaf.*

**KEY**

 Oak

 Scots pine

 Cherry

 Common crab apple

 Birch

 Hazel

 *Rosa alba*

 Wayfaring tree

 Common dogwood

 Native privet

 Common hawthorn

 Hedge

 Bulbs

 Perennials, biennials, annuals

Long grass

Short grass

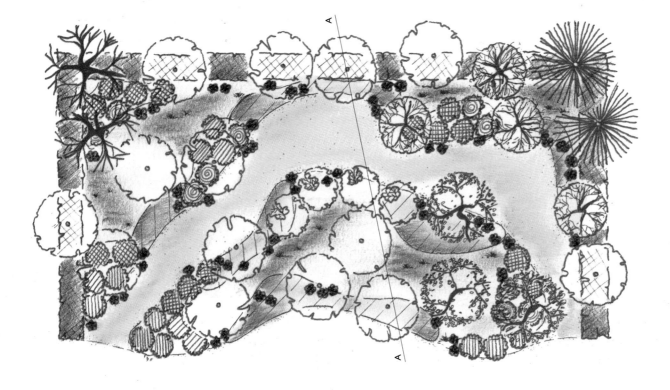

free-draining, poor, thin, limestone soil, wild cherry does extremely well. It has many advantages, the first being its growth rate, the second the autumn colour, the third its showy blossoms and the fourth its medium height. If I had a damp soil I would opt for alders as a nurse crop as these tolerate degrees of wetness that no other tree apart from willow can stand and grow very fast.

### THE SHRUB LAYER
The shrub layer contributes greatly to the shady, enclosed character required and can be used to screen out unwanted views. An informal boundary of native shrubs such as *Rosa canina* (dog rose), *Viburnum opulus* (guelder rose), *Crataegus monogyna* (hawthorn) and *Ligustrum vulgare* (wild privet) will provide a rich habitat and additional shelter, colour and shadow. Throughout your woodland patch, intersperse other groups of native shrubs like

*ABOVE LEFT The path through some young woodland has been surfaced with bark, a sympathetic and economical material that is ideal both for children's demands and for general use.*
*ABOVE CENTRE Stepping stones are laid in a diamond pattern through an area of ornamental woodland.*
*ABOVE RIGHT A temporary twig fence forms a pretty barrier to protect the carefully nurtured wild flowers planted in the long grass meadow.*

hazel, holly or box and use them to help define a woody walk.

### MANAGEMENT
When the mixed planting has started to produce the form you want and plants are becoming overcrowded, you can start to manicure the woodland. Coppicing – repeatedly cutting trees or shrubs down to ground level – means that sunlight is let in and new plants will establish themselves in those open patches. The harvested wood is often useful, and the coppiced plant will respond by throwing up lots of new stems to form a multi-stemmed tree. Coppiced hazel woodland, traditionally grown to produce thin poles for useful items such as hurdles and beanpoles, has gone out of vogue because of the labour costs, but on a small scale in a family garden it is ideal. Many other trees can be coppiced, especially ash, sweet chestnut, birch and willow. If you coppice a few trees after 8–12 years, then coppice a different batch two years later when the growth has thickened up, you will maintain the overall habitat. About eight years after you started, repeat the cycle.

Do not forget the lower storey, where you can plant foxgloves, *Silene dioica* (red campion), *Polygonatum multiflorum* (Solomon's seal) and *Hyacinthoides non-scriptus* (bluebell) as soon as there is enough shade to inhibit the growth of grass.

# Establishing a Woodland Garden

Once you have chosen the plants for your woodland garden, you have to decide exactly how you are going to establish them. If you are going to plant a native mixed hedge border (*see page 140*) or a coppice along the lines of that on page 136 in an area of existing grass, you will first need to mark out on the ground the positions of the tree and hedge planting, using canes and string. This will help you to visualize your garden and allow you to make any adjustments to your design before you start digging.

## PLANTING DISTANCES

To obtain the quick results usually required you must plant the trees approximately 2m (6½ft) apart. For a natural effect the spacing should vary somewhat – maybe 1m (3¼ft) in one place and 3m (10ft) elsewhere. This may seem close, but in 10 years or so you can start to thin them out if required.

## BUYING TREES

As to the size of tree to plant, the smaller the better. Bare-rooted transplants of 45–60cm (1½–2ft) high are extremely cheap and will establish far quicker than a large standard, which takes time to recover from being up-rooted and replanted. A second point is that the established appearance of these smaller trees is more natural, as the major upset given to transplanted standards alters the final form and shape. You may have to ask your garden centre to get you these smaller plants to order as larger specimens with a better mark-up are the norm. The maximum size I would use is 1.2m (4ft).

It is a common misconception that by buying container-grown trees you can use larger plants without them suffering from transplantation. In fact, research has shown that container plants establish far less quickly than bare-rooted ones. This is because the near-

perfect medium provided in their containers makes the roots reluctant to leave it, and they tend not to strike out into new ground. Also, container-grown trees are originally grown in the ground and then lifted and put into containers approximately one or two seasons before selling, and so are often 'disturbed' plants anyway.

## CULTIVATION

In the first few growing seasons the predominant factor influencing your trees' growth is moisture, so forget the fertilizer initially – just make sure that they have enough to drink. It is often not feasible to water trees, but as long as you ensure that no weeds or grass are growing around the base of their stems to compete for moisture they will probably be fine. If you grow trees with mown grass around their trunks during establishment (the first three or four years) their growth rate will be 60–70

*These illustrations show the development of section AA on page 136. 1–3 years: Plant small transplants and protect them from rabbits with spiral guards. Keep the ground around the base free of grass and weeds to reduce competition for moisture. 7–10 years: The trees will be producing light shade, so start to introduce wild flowers and ground cover. Remove vigorous weeds if they become a problem. 15–20 years: At this point you may want to thin out some trees. Characterful trees with bent trunks add to the woodland's charm.*

1-3 YEARS

7-10 YEARS

per cent slower than those grown with bare earth around their roots, simply because they are obtaining less water.

A painless way to remove weed competition is to put a tree spat around the base of the tree when planting. These are 450–900cm (1½–3ft) squares of thick black polythene, polypropylene, bituminous felt or wool matting, which are anchored by digging in the corners. They can also be obtained in long runs for hedges. A 50–75mm (2–3in) thick layer of very coarse bark mulch could be used instead, but all perennial weeds would have to be removed first.

Chemical control works well if you have no objections to using chemicals. Before planting, apply glyphosate or a similar non-selective, non-residual, systemic weedkiller to a 1m (3¼ft) diameter patch around the site where the tree will grow or along entire hedge runs, and most perennial weeds will be removed. After planting you could control further weed growth by applying a thick mulch or putting old newspapers on the soil and covering them with grass clippings, compost or other debris to conceal them.

Little trees will not need staking, and in fact staking hinders their growth by producing a stem which is thicker above the tie than at the ground and restricting the root movement that is needed to produce a well-branched fibrous root system.

Rabbits like to gnaw young bark, killing the tree. To prevent this, put plastic spiral tree guards around the base, an easy and inexpensive procedure. Some trees dislike exposure, and individual shelters (usually made from heavy polythene and mesh) can be put round them to assist their growth initially.

### PLANTING THE UNDERSTOREY

Once your trees and shrubs are established (3-4 years) moisture competition is not as critical, as their roots are probably into good water sources deeper down. This is the time to introduce the understorey. The range available here is so great that it is a matter of personal preference. You may decide to have no grass apart from mown pathways, which over the years will get shaded out and could then be replaced by bark. Sheets of *Hedera* (ivy), interspersed with patches of *Primula vulgaris* (common primrose), *Anemone nemorosa* (wood anemone), *Allium ursinum* (wild garlic), *Convallaria majalis* (lily-of-the-valley) and ferns are just a few of the available plants that will make your woodland look authentic; a wildflower catalogue will guide your choice. Position your plants in the shadier spaces, control the competition and let them spread with the shade.

### MANAGING THE WOODLAND

When you are managing the woodland, keep long-term aims in view. Your ultimate goal is unlikely to be a single-species copse with tall, straight-trunked trees as required for timber production, but rather an area of dappled shade with some character and charm. Maybe you will train a tree to grow at a leaning angle or bend two over to form an archway. When thinning the trees, you may decide to pull out a perfect example with a single, strong leader and keep a forked specimen instead so that you can fit a tree house into it in a few years.

15-20 YEARS

# Hedges and Borders

A common choice of plants for hedging is a line of non-indigenous conifers to form a dense boundary. However, a native hedgerow composed of a range of plants to suit the conditions such as hawthorn, viburnum, native privet, holly and dog rose will support an infinitely greater variety of wildlife as well as providing colour and interest with berries, flowers, budding shoots and autumn leaves, not to mention the scores of plants which will thrive along the hedgerow base. The visual screen it will provide during the summer can be every bit as good as that given by conifers as well as looking a good deal more in harmony with the landscape. If you require more privacy in winter you can simply increase the amounts of holly and wild privet.

A mixed hedge such as this will not reach the heights of many conifer hedges, but this can be a bonus. If height is required, intersperse some hedgerow trees, which will contribute an additional tier of foliage towards the desired woodland edge effect (*see page 136*). This multiple canopy allows you to fit in more plants and create an interesting, rich and varied habitat which will go a little way towards helping to replace all those thousands of acres of woodland that are steadily being ripped out.

## PLANTING

When planting a border, try to pack in as many plants as you can that will attract butterflies. The presence of some dazzling peacocks, holly

| PLANT | SOIL SUITABILITY | | |
|---|---|---|---|
| | Wet | Normal | Dry |
| Acer campestre<br>Field maple | | Normal | Dry |
| Cornus sanguinea<br>Common dogwood | Wet | Normal | |
| Crataegus monogyna<br>Common hawthorn | Wet | Normal | |
| Euonymous europaeus<br>Spindle | Wet | Normal | Dry |
| Hippophae rhamnoides<br>Sea buckthorn | Wet | Normal | Dry |
| Ilex aquifolium<br>Common holly | | Normal | Dry |

| PLANT | SOIL SUITABILITY | | |
|---|---|---|---|
| | Wet | Normal | Dry |
| Ligustrum vulgare<br>Common privet | | Normal | Dry |
| Rhamnus catharticus<br>Common buckthorn | | Normal | Dry |
| Rhamnus frangula<br>Alder buckthorn | | Normal | Dry |
| Rosa canina<br>Dog rose | | Normal | Dry |
| Viburnum lantana<br>Wayfaring tree | | Normal | Dry |
| Viburnum opulus<br>Guelder rose | Wet | Normal | |

*This selection includes many common native hedging plants which will tolerate the conditions indicated in the chart. For a really stout hedge plant a fairly high proportion of hawthorn and only use a sprinkling of dog rose for decoration.*

**PLANTING PLAN FOR WET SOILS**

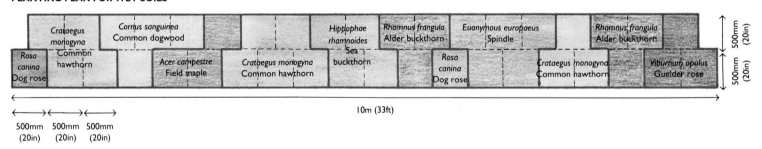

**PLANTING PLAN FOR DRY SOILS**

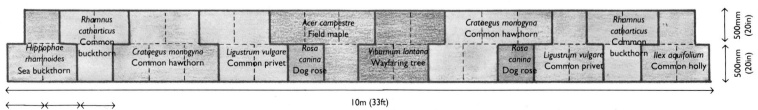

blues and painted ladies will really bring your garden to life, and you will be doing your bit to preserve species that are being driven to the edge of extinction as chemical spraying destroys their habitats. Mauve and purple plants, such as buddlejas, lilac, lavender, valerian and *Eupatorium purpureum*, hold a special attraction for butterflies, as do native and commonly naturalized plants, such as *Viburnum lantana* (wayfaring tree), *V. opulus* (guelder rose), *Ajuga reptans* (bugle), *Dipsacus fullonum* (teasel), and *Hesperis matronalis* (sweet rocket). For bees, plant *Cistus* spp. (rock roses), *Laurus nobilis* (bay), potentillas, spiraea, *Viburnum tinus* and foxgloves.

## MAINTENANCE

If you do not wish to change the mixture of plants in your borders, try a more sympathetic maintenance regime. Instead of chopping all

your herbaceous plants down in the autumn, leave the stems there so that hollow stalks will provide a habitat for many insects. When spring comes, cut the stalks down to allow the new growth to emerge unimpeded and chop them up to form a mulch over the soil.

*ABOVE This colourful border is packed with plants to attract a variety of insects, and is sited in a sunny, sheltered position to enhance its value to butterflies. Plan a border which will flower very early and also very late (annuals are useful here) and include flowers with edible seedheads.*

*LEFT Fences can be a rich habitat for wildlife. If you fix trellis to a fence make sure there is a gap between the two as this is an ideal refuge.*

Mulches are excellent time-savers, reducing the amount of weeds able to germinate and keeping the moisture in the ground through dry summers. They also provide a good habitat for insects. Avoid fine bark mulches, which look good but are an excellent germinating medium for weeds and also absorb moisture so that in dry periods plant roots grow towards this damp area rather than forming a healthy deep root system.

# Pets in the Garden

Most children yearn for a pet of some sort and indeed many families feel life's not complete without a furred or feathered companion or two. Pets can mean damaged borders and unsightly hutches and runs, but with a bit of forethought the pleasures will far outweigh the pain. The possibility of disease is also a concern for parents, but simple precautions can make it a remote one (*see box*).

## DOGS

In terms of playmates for children, dogs cannot be beaten – they will usually join enthusiastically in any activity, particularly if it involves running, jumping and scrambling. For a keen gardener, though, the top priority is to teach dogs not to go on, or dig in, borders. This message can usually be got across in one afternoon's weeding spent with a new puppy. It may be ignored in moments of excitement but once they are past that first flush of puppyish exuberance (usually at about nine months) dogs will rarely step on borders again.

## CATS

All a cat really asks from a garden is somewhere to sharpen its claws and a sunny spot in which to snooze. However, some clumps of *Nepeta × faassenii* (catmint) as a bonus will send most cats dizzy with delight. For a homemade version of the catnip mice that are sold in pet

*A bird table like this allows you to hang food from it as well as placing it on the table. To prevent the build-up of disease, move the table annually.*

shops you can dry some *Nepeta*, sew it into a piece of cloth and tie a length of string to it. The children will enjoy dragging it around the garden to entice the cat into some action.

## RABBITS

Rabbits come in a range of varieties from standard bunnies to lop-eared, plush-coated creatures that wouldn't look out of place on a soft toy counter. The simple solution to rabbit runs cluttering up the garden is to build one that you like looking at, such as the one on pages 144–5. A small area in the corner of the garden with all the paraphernalia such as food bins and winter hutches screened from sight gives children some scope for organizing their 'pets' corner' in the way they want.

## CHICKENS

Chickens are fascinating to watch as they scratch around and they have the added bonus of providing truly fresh eggs. Their only drawback is that they are partial to certain plants, particularly hostas and lettuces. The best plan is to confine them to a pen for most of the day during the growing season and allow them a freer run in the winter months.

---

## *Preventing Disease*

**MYXOMATOSIS**
This disease affects rabbits only.
**Prevention**
Inoculate pet rabbits against it to prevent infection from wild rabbits.

**TOXOCARIASIS**
Eggs of the roundworm *Toxocara* passed in faeces of infected dogs can contaminate children's hands. If eggs are swallowed there is a slight possibility of toxocariasis, which usually only causes slight flu-like

symptoms. In rare cases vision may be impaired; total blindness is rarer still.
**Prevention**
Worm puppies at two weeks old and at least four more times before they are six months; train them to soil in a specific area and tell your children to avoid this patch of the garden. Worm adult dogs at least every six months. Freshly passed faeces are not a toxocariasis hazard as the eggs take two to three weeks to mature, so clean up all dog faeces regularly. Remind the children to wash their hands after playing with pets. If you inherit a garden from a dog-owner, bear in mind that *Toxocara* eggs can live for up to three years.

**TOXOPLASMOSIS**
Toxoplasmosis is caused by a tiny parasite, *Toxoplasma gondii*, found in most animals and birds, in garden soil and on fresh vegetables. Cats excrete *Toxoplasma* eggs in their faeces if they pick up an infection from wild birds, mice or raw meat. Toxoplasmosis is not usually dangerous to healthy adults or children, but if a woman catches it for the first time while she is pregnant the infection may damage the sight and brain of the foetus and/or cause epilepsy.
**Prevention**
Pregnant women should wear gloves when gardening or handling cat litter/faeces and wash hands afterwards. Cover sandpits to prevent cats using them.

*TOP LEFT Chickens are productive pets and simple to look after. They become extremely tame and usually mix well with rabbits and guinea pigs. Restrict them to the informal areas of the garden.*

*TOP CENTRE This kennel has been designed to blend in with the stone walls of the house — an attention to detail which also means it is beautifully cool and comfortable for the dog in summer.*

*TOP RIGHT A dovecote is a fascinating focal point. This freestanding version stands out well against foliage; a wall-mounted one will transform a blank end wall of a building.*

*ABOVE Dogs are deservedly one of the most popular pets, and with discipline can easily be taught to stay away from borders and ornamental pools. Prevent disease by regular worming.*

# PROJECT: A RABBIT HUTCH/CHICKEN RUN

This attractive run is designed for rabbits and guinea pigs, though it could comfortably be used for a couple of bantams or small chickens, in which case a nesting box and perch should be added in the covered part, making sure it gives them enough headroom.

## YOU WILL NEED

- One sheet of 19mm (¾in) WBP (exterior grade) plywood, 1220 x 2440mm (48 x 96in), to form four arches, three roof braces, and two doors and adjacent uprights
- Two sheets of 6mm (¼in) WBP plywood, 1220 x 2440mm (48 x 96in), to form the floor and cladding strips (and beam compass)
- Six lengths of hardwood dowelling, 690mm (27⅛in) x 19mm (¾in) diameter
- Two horizontal base beams, 25 x 50 x 2026mm (1 x 2 x 79¾in), hardwood or tanalized softwood
- Four arch braces, 25 x 50 x 820mm (1 x 2 x 32¼in), hardwood or tanalized softwood
- Chicken netting, 8m (26ft 3in) x 900mm (36in) wide
- One turn button
- One door bolt, 63mm (2½in) long
- Weatherproof woodworking adhesive
- 25mm (1in) x 1.8mm (¹⁄₁₆in) galvanized wire nails
- 15mm (⅝in) x 1.6mm (¹⁄₁₆in) galvanized staples
- 38mm (1½in) x No 8 zinc-plated woodscrews
- Non-toxic wood stain (dark brown)

**Tools**
- Jigsaw • Plane • Hammer • Drill and wood bits • Tenon saw • Screwdriver • Wire cutters or tin snips • Panel saw • Try square

## MARKING OUT THE FRAME

Start by making a template for the central roof brace by taping a piece of card the size of the surrounding rectangle across one end of a plywood sheet. Make a beam compass from a strip of 6mm (¼in) plywood, with a nail through one end and holes for a pencil at radii of 2100 and 2025mm (82⅝ and 79⅝in) from it. Use this to mark the curves.

Mark out the arches on the plywood, following the cutting plan. Mark the centre line of each arch, both for marking the curves and to help in positioning the roof braces later. Cut the beam compass down to a more manageable length for the arch radii of 410mm and 360mm (16⅛ and 14⅛in). The partition arch is solid except for the access hole, which must be large enough to let through the future occupant. Position it to one side (but not closer than 75mm/3in to the edge) to leave a relatively draught-proof area on the other side.

Mark out the rectangles for the roof braces and mark the 70° angled ends on the side braces, either using a protractor or by measuring in from the ends of the rectangle. Use the template to mark on the curves; those on the side braces are offset within the rectangles. The side braces are mirror images of each other, so make them identical and turn one of them end over end when fitting it.

Cut out the marked components close to the lines to leave undamaged plywood for the doors and their supports. Smooth all edges with medium glasspaper.

## ASSEMBLING THE FRAME

Glue and screw the four arch braces to one face of each arch, with the 50mm (2in) face against the plywood. Lay the two horizontal base beams flat on the ground, parallel to each other, and with the inner edges 720mm (28⅜in) apart. Set up the arches squarely on the base beams, with the flat face of the small arches flush with the ends of the beams, and the large arches spaced 630mm (24¾in) away from them so that their braces face away from the centre. (There should be 690mm/27⅛in between the large arches.) Glue and screw them to the beams.

Position the central roof brace with its thickness centred on the marked centre line of the two large arches and the outer curve flush with their top edges. Glue and screw it in place with two screws into each end. Offset the side roof braces from the central one sufficiently to allow the screws to be inserted, then fix them in the same way.

Cut out the hutch floor 630 x 820mm (24¾ x 32¼in) from 6mm (¼in) plywood and then nail it to the arch braces in the partition arch section.

To maintain the shape of the netting in the middle section, cut six lengths of 19mm (¾in) diameter dowelling to span the gap between the large arches. Glue and screw the dowelling at equal distances round the arches.

## FITTING THE DOORS

The two doors overlap the end arch by 25mm (1in). Cut them to a height of 625mm (24½in) with a top radius of 385mm (15⅛in). Cut the two uprights, 25 x 240mm (1 x 9½in), to take the vertical hinge flaps, and glue and screw them to the small arch, flush with the outer and bottom edges. Screw the hinges to the doors and fix them to the uprights with one screw per hinge, to check for fit. Plane down the long edges as necessary, then refix.

Screw the turn button 12mm (½in) in from the edge of one door and screw the bolt to the inside of the same door so that it just clears the floor in the raised position. Screw a small

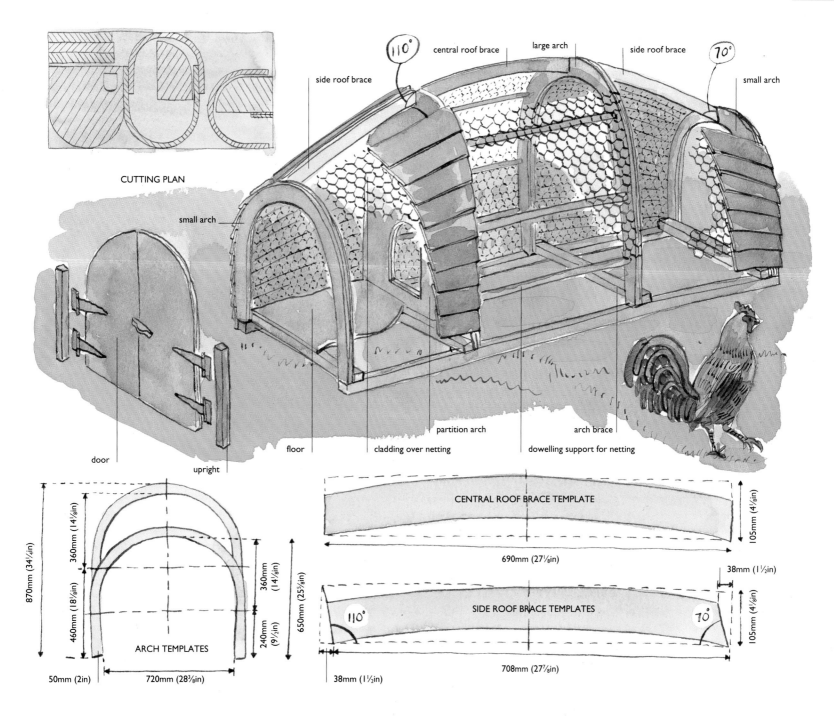

CUTTING PLAN

small arch

door

upright

110° central roof brace    large arch    side roof brace    70°

side roof brace    small arch

floor    partition arch    arch brace

cladding over netting    dowelling support for netting

870mm (34¼in)

360mm (14⅛in)

460mm (18⅛in)

360mm (14⅛in)

240mm (9½in)

650mm (25⅝in)

ARCH TEMPLATES

50mm (2in)    720mm (28⅜in)

CENTRAL ROOF BRACE TEMPLATE

105mm (4⅛in)

690mm (27⅛in)

38mm (1½in)

110°    SIDE ROOF BRACE TEMPLATES    70°

105mm (4⅛in)

708mm (27⅞in)

38mm (1½in)

plywood block to the face of the arch brace and drill a hole in it to take the bolt.

## COVERING THE FRAMEWORK

Apply two coats of preservative woodstain to all assembled components first; you could also paint one face of the 6mm (¼in) plywood to give added protection to the cladding.

Cut chicken netting to cover the top and one end, to prevent rabbits from eating the cladding. For chickens, just cover the middle section and end. Pleat the netting over the end sections, so that it lies flat, and fix it to all edges of the frame with galvanized staples.

Cut 90 x 800mm (3½ x 31½in) strips of 6mm (¼in) plywood, along the length of the sheets, for cladding the two end sections of the frame. Starting at the bottom, nail the strips to the arches; trim all ends flush, except round the doors where they should

project by 10mm (⅜in). Overlap each previous strip by 30mm (1¼in) at the outer end and 10mm (⅜in) at the inner end. Cover the gap at the top with a trapezium of plywood, 740 mm (29⅛in) long, with ends 140 and 180mm (5½ and 7in) wide (or of a size to suit), nailed to the arches and the side roof braces.

Paint the hutch with two coats of non-toxic preservative woodstain, allowing the odour to wear off completely before using the run.

# THE
# PLANTING
# SCHEME

*Planting to please every member of the family requires*

*careful selection and planning if the garden is to fulfil*

*the many functions demanded of it. Some areas may*

*call for tough plants that will survive ball games, den-*

*making and general hurly-burly relatively unscathed,*

*while others will need to be sufficiently interesting and*

*attractive to satisfy the horticulturally minded.*

# Planting designs

Gardeners frequently have problems with the arrangement of the plants in their borders. They are often dissatisfied with the overall result but do not know how to rectify it. Undoubtedly it is a complex business, for not only must plants thrive in the conditions that prevail in your garden, but they must also perform as part of an orchestrated sequence so that the whole border looks good through the changing seasons.

### FIRST IMPRESSIONS

Common reasons for borders falling short of the mark is that they look spotty, incohesive and lack a definite style. To prevent this happening in your garden borders, concentrate on the overall impression and character you want to create in each different section of the garden before you start to think about which particular plants to grow. For example, decide whether you want a pastel-coloured cottage garden feel, a bold tropical effect or a colour-led theme and plant accordingly.

### A PLANTING PLAN

Having established the style of planting you are aiming for, set about producing a plan. In the illustrations opposite you can see three different ways to plan a border. In the first example, the strong co-ordinating element is the low box hedge planted to divide the bed into a pattern of triangles. The same grouping of three shrubs fills the centre of each triangle, with adjacent groups of smaller shrubs. Additional interest has been given by repeated clumps of different herbaceous plants. Depending on the height you choose to clip the box hedge, and the choice of plants, the bed could look smart and neatly trimmed, or informal, with laxer growing plants softening and breaking up the lines of the hedges. Topiary could be used to punctuate the planting groups and add further interest, particularly in winter.

The second illustration shows a more traditional approach. Here a longer stretch of planting has been broken up and planted alternately with two different groups of plants (A and B). This gives a long border a definite unity. More than two groups could be repeated or, if you find the replication of the whole group too repetitive in a shorter border, just repeat certain elements, such as one group of shrubs and two distinctive groups of

*This garden exudes an exciting subtropical air not only through the use of bold-foliaged plants such as the 'hardy' banana* Musa basjoo, *which will survive out-of-doors all year round in temperate zones with the protection of hessian covering during cold snaps.*

*The carefully controlled but apparently natural feel of this garden is achieved through skilful planting with a wonderful use of colour. Many of these plants self seed, a characteristic which quickly gives a new garden a look of maturity and also provides exciting new developments from year to year.*

**PLANTING PLANS**

*Plants must be carefully placed in a border even if the look you wish you achieve is wild and natural. A strong pattern is provided by a low clipped hedge, punctuated with repeated groups of shrubs (top). A long border alternates two complementary groups of plants, A and B, along its length (centre). A wild, jungle effect is achieved by studied 'random' planting (bottom).*

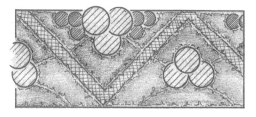

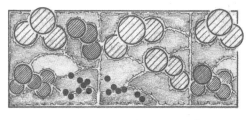

A        B        A

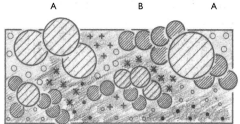

**KEY**

 Shrubs

Perennials

 Perennials, biennials and annuals

Bulbs

herbaceous plants. Ensure that the choice of repeating plants enhances the character you wish to evoke.

The third illustration shows a much more random approach to the planting plan. Here groups of larger plants have been dotted intermittently through areas of lower plants. Some of these are accent plants, with bold, eye-catching foliage or flowers contrasting with more neutral neighbours. The result is a lush jungle effect; to maintain cohesion, repeat groups of plants and use self-seeding varieties which will appear informally throughout the border filling any unplanted spaces. This planting plan would be ideal for a wilder part of the garden.

**INSTANT IMPACT**

When you plant a new border, ensure that it looks reasonably full as soon as possible. Propagate or purchase several of each species and do not be afraid to plant them close together. The only possible downside is that in periods of drought the competition for moisture is greater, but you can water well to compensate. Otherwise, as a temporary measure, fill the gaps with annuals or quick-to-establish fillers that are easy to propagate yourself, such as *Alchemilla mollis* (lady's mantle), *Nepeta* (catmint) and *Senecio* Dunedin Hybrid 'Sunshine'. In due course you may pull them out once the more choice players start to come into their own.

**ENJOY THE PLANNING PROCESS**

Finally, planting design is not that easy a challenge, given the many variables to consider. However, do not despair. While you might not get it right all the time, that is half the fun of gardening – trying different types of plants in different places to create different effects. Although the structure of the garden and choice of hard landscaping materials are important, it is the plants that add the dramatic, dynamic element to a garden, constantly changing as they grow and develop through the seasons and years. Regular re-appraisal of your garden plantings will allow you to try new and exciting combinations in areas which seem to be flagging.

# Tough Plants for Play

The joy of gardening for me and many adults is focused mainly around plants, and the damage caused to them by stray balls, children's feet and pet dogs can be heart-breaking. However, an alternative to banishing children from these treasured areas is to plant up certain parts of the garden with child-friendly plants. These patches will become the children's domain in which they can trample undergrowth, dig holes, whittle stems, pick flowers for their tree house and make dens to their hearts' content.

## THE SHRUB WILLOWS

Ideal for this purpose are the shrub willows; several varieties have striking coloured stems which appeal to children, and they establish quickly creating an ideal den-making environment. Perhaps their best feature is that they grow back rapidly after being damaged. Some of the best are *Salix alba* 'Chermesina', with bright red stems, *Salix alba vitellina*, the attractive yellow-stemmed variety, and *Salix daphnoides*, with dark purple stems. It is the young shoots which display the brightest coloration, so cut the old stems back to about 15cm (6in) every other year in late spring after the winter display. The new shoots will emerge rapidly. *Salix elaeagnos* (hoary willow) is one of my favourites, with its delicate, narrow, silver-green leaves. Although a little less vigorous, it is still up to the job. All willows like moisture but will still thrive in dry soil.

## BAMBOO JUNGLES

A large thicket of the more vigorous bamboo creates an instant mini-jungle and as a result

## *Tough Plant Directory*

### SHRUBS AND TREES

**Bamboo** The taller bamboos (*Pseudosasa japonica* and *Fargesia spathacea*) provide clumps and thickets for dens. Most are hardy but dislike high winds and drought. *Pseudosasa japonica* is most tolerant of heavy play but is invasive, and can look lacklustre; *Fargesia spathacea* and *F. nitida* spread more slowly but have elegant foliage.

**Buddleja (butterfly bush)** Rapidly growing plants which bloom quickly with brightly coloured spires and attract butterflies. Buddleja recovers from damage; *B. davidii* 'Royal Red' is a stunning colour.

**Cornus (dogwood)** Useful plants, which establish fast; in winter the young stems of several varieties are a bright colour. *Cornus alba* 'Elegantissima' is less vigorous for small spaces, and has attractive white and green leaves.

**Cortaderia (pampas grass)** This looks at its best in groups of 3–5; *C. selloana* 'Sunningdale Silver' grows up to 3–4m (10–13ft) high, with silver plumes.

**Corylus avellana (native hazel)** A small hazel thicket provides a play environment and a supply of sticks for supporting peas and making archways.

**Eleaegnus x ebbingei** This is a fast tough evergreen with a dense habit that responds well to cutting back.

**Hypericum** All the hypericums recover well from damage. *H.* 'Hidcote' has a compact habit, giving dense wood for forming tunnels in. It has large, saucer-shaped yellow flowers over a long period.

**Kerria** Tall, graceful shrubs with green stems, which spread readily by suckers. *K. japonica* 'Pleniflora' has double, rich yellow flowers and arching branches.

**Lavatera thuringiaca (mallow)** Fast-growing elegant shrubs with greyish, downy stems and leaves; flowers produced from summer to late autumn.

**Ligustrum (privet)** These recover well after rough treatment. *Ligustrum vulgare* (native privet) is partially evergreen and more open than *Ligustrum ovalifolium*.

**Prunus laurocerasus (common laurel)** This large shrub can grow into a small tree although it responds well to cutting back. As well as providing good material to play in, it forms a fast-growing evergreen screen.

**Salix (willow)** Open shrubs which recover well after rough treatment. To maintain the bright stem colour, cut back hard each second year. *S. alba* 'Chermesina' (scarlet willow) – the young stems are scarlet; *S. alba vitellina* (golden willow) – bright yellow young stems; *S. elaeagnos* (hoary willow) – linear silver leaves clothing slender stems; *S. daphnoides* (violet willow) – the purple young stems often have a white bloom.

**Sambucus (elder)** Quick to establish and tolerant of most conditions. Avoid the common elder as it is rather coarse in appearance and seeds prolifically. *S. nigra* 'Aurea' (golden elder) – the golden leaves are very bright; *Sambucus nigra* 'Purpurea' (purple-leaved elder) – the young leaves are flushed purple.

**Symphoricarpus** These are quite hardy and are suited to dry shade among trees. *S. albus* (snowberry) forms dense clumps ideal for secret dens.

**Viburnum lantana (wayfaring tree)** A native hedgerow plant which recovers well from damage; creamy white flowers in late spring to early summer.

### GROUND-COVER PLANTS

**Hedera (ivy)** Many of the ivies form good dense ground cover, and are economical and quick to establish. *H. hibernica* (Irish ivy) is a good example.

**Vinca major (periwinkle)** This forms attractive swathes of ground cover and has bright blue flowers, although it can become invasive.

**Euonymus** Many form good ground cover and come in different tones of green, gold, white and cream. They vary in height and vigour. *E. fortunei* 'Silver Queen' is fairly slow to establish and will also tend to climb. *E.* 'Emerald Gaiety' has a more open habit and establishes slightly faster.

*A well-established clump of bamboo provides ample scope for den-making. Through the woven entrance of this secret lair lies a network of tunnels and rooms fulfilling every child's dream, while informal planting in the foreground allows the play area to blend easily into the cultivated part of the garden.*

holds endless possibilities for children (but beware, they do make excellent spears). The most suitable varieties are those with a tendency towards thuggish behaviour, such as *Pseudosasa japonica* which is an adaptable beast, forming canes up to 4.5m (15ft) high, or sometimes even 6m (20ft). It bears lush masses of glossy green leaves up to 30cm (12in) long. The other two shortlisted species are *Fargesia spathacea* and *F. nitida*. Neither are as high nor vigorous as *Pseudosasa japonica*, reaching heights in the region of 3m (10ft), nor are they as tolerant of dry exposed conditions, but they are more graceful plants.

## QUICK-RECOVERY PLANTS
The tree mallows grow at a terrific rate and a pretty one is *Lavatera thuringiaca* 'Barnsley', with pale pink flowers. They all grow easily from cuttings at phenomenal speeds, and flower non-stop throughout the spring and summer months given a suitable, sunny site.

*Cornus* (dogwood), *Corylus avenana* (native hazel), *Ligustrum* (privet), *Prunus laurocerasus* (common laurel), *Sambucus* (elder) and *Symphoricarpus* are all easy to establish and recover quickly after being damaged. For smaller gardens, *Hypericum* 'Hidcote' is useful, growing to just over 1m (3¼ft) high with a spread of a little less. This plant is ideal for making tunnels in! All the hebes are renowned for their powers of recovery after rough play, though the taller ones such as *H.* 'Midsummer Beauty' and *H. brachysiphon* give more scope for creating secret worlds.

## ADDING ORNAMENTAL INTEREST
In the foreground of these tough plant beds, establish drifts of prolific self-seeders such as the white foxglove, *Digitalis purpurea alba*, *Verbascum olympicum* (mullein) with its soft yellow flowers, *Angelica archangelica*, *Lunaria annua variegata* (variegated honesty), *Hesperis matrionalis* (sweet rocket), or *Centranthus ruber*

*albus* (white valerian). These set seed freely, so the odd plant can be trampled underfoot.

## PROVIDING GROUND COVER
The play area will look more attractive if the soil is covered. In summer this will be taken care of by the self-seeding plants, but the simplest method to maintain the cover through winter is a good layer of coarse-grade bark. This is an added draw for children, helps to keep weeds down and preserves soil moisture. Alternatively a vigorous ground coverer such as *Vinca major* (periwinkle), *Hedera hibernica* (the ground-cover ivy that is less prone to climb), *Aegopodium podagraria* 'Variegatum' (variegated ground elder) or any of the more vigorous evergreen varieties of *Euonymus*, such as *E.* 'Emerald Gaiety', will increase the level of interest. All these plants will recover quickly after damage. If you are limited in terms of space, avoid the rampant growers, particularly the variegated ground elder.

# Barrier Plants

Any well-used and much enjoyed family garden can get rather knocked about from time to time. And although much of the charm of a family garden comes from that well-used and much-lived-in look, I am as neurotic as the next gardener about my favourite plants being bashed about by footballs, flying boomerangs, model aeroplanes, excitable dogs, racing feet and the like.

## A BARRIER FOR DELICATE PLANTS

The best way to achieve flourishing borders in these circumstances is to site the more delicate plants away from the main zone of robust activity, as there is nothing more tedious than to be continually nagging and watching out for 'accidental' destruction. If your garden is too small for this, then site the more delicate plants behind a protective layer of toughies. In my garden, the choice borders have a low hedge of box, which clearly demarcates the front edge of the border and forms the start of a 'no go zone'. Any flying missile which lands in there, stays there, until special clearance is

*Strategically sited containers provide a strong linking rhythm along the length of the border and also clearly define the edge discouraging close play and thus protecting the vulnerable plants behind. The paving allows plants to flop over the edge of the border without hindering mowing.*

granted. I chose to plant *Buxus sempervirens*, not the dwarf hedging box, *Buxus* 'Suffruticosa' which would have taken too long to create an effective barrier. The former quickly forms a thick, robust hedge and is very easy to propagate from cuttings, although they take about 9–12 months to root. The hedge needs to be clipped twice a year to keep it looking neat.

## OPTIONS FOR BORDER EDGING

Box-edged borders, though, are not to everyone's taste. For a slightly more relaxed look, *Hebe anomala* is excellent and grows quickly to form a good hedge; it also regenerates well if knocked about a bit. For an informal and colourful hedge, the larger potentillas work well, although the plants behind them must be at least 1m (3ft) high, otherwise they will be hidden away. Do not forget that the front

*Two bold groups of* Phormium and bamboo *clearly define two potentially vulnerable corners. These useful and attractive plants will stand their ground well if small undisciplined feet try to impinge on their territory, and at the same time create a lush, jungle feel.*

edge of the border need not form a straight line. Box edging may also follow a strong, scalloped line or a gentle curve.

## CHOOSING TOUGHER PLANTS

If you do not want to define borders with a hedge, then simply fill the more vulnerable front areas in the beds with plants from the list opposite. Most of these are fairly common and their popularity stems from the fact that they are easy-to-grow, reliable plants that perform well and shoot back quickly after being trampled on. The planting can be spiced up with strategically sited additions of less tough, but more eye-catching good performers.

## CORNERS OF FLOWER BEDS

Other characteristically vulnerable places in a garden are the corners of flower beds, which can become battered by bikes, buggies and balls. Make sure that you choose sturdy plants for such areas. In my childhood, we had one such vulnerable corner where a large, vigorous dark red double peony grew. Despite being repeatedly jumped over, around and through, the

# Barrier plant directory

Plants from the Tough Plant Directory (*see page 150*) could be used in addition to the ones below.

## SHRUBS

***Buxus sempervirens*** (box) is a large species which can also be used as a low hedge. It will need clipping twice a year, but it establishes much faster and forms a more robust barrier than the commonly used *B.* 'Suffruticosa'. A neat, low hedge can be formed from cuttings in three to four years.

***B.* 'Suffruticosa'** (box) is a useful edging plant but is slow to get going. Clipping once a year should be enough for this box.

***Cotoneaster*** varieties will all grow back well after being damaged, and come in all shapes and sizes from ground-hugging to small trees; some are evergreen.

***Erica*** (heaths and heathers) includes well-foliaged 'cushions' which will soon re-grow after misuse.

***Escallonia*** varieties are useful fillers.

***Hebe*** varieties grow back well following damage, provided that they are young, healthy specimens. They are good, quick-growing fillers to use while waiting for more exciting plants to mature. The plants are easy to propagate from cuttings.

***Lonicera nitida*** is a fast growing, tough, evergreen filler.

***L. n.* 'Baggesen's Gold'** (honeysuckle) is not as sturdy as the plant described above but its vivid, yellow evergreen foliage will tolerate abuse.

***Mahonia aquifolium*** is a useful, evergreen plant which spreads by suckers. It tolerates poor soils and has fragrant yellow flowers in spring.

***Potentilla*** varieties are excellent plants which can be used for low-growing hedges. They flower for long periods and tolerate poor soils.

***Pyracantha* 'Soleil d'Or'** is a useful, spreading evergreen with yellow berries.

***Rubus cockburnianus*** (blackberry) has strong, arching stems with a purplish white bloom.

***R. tricolor*** (blackberry) is an evergreen which spreads like wild fire, so be warned.

***Senecio Dunedin Hybrid* 'Sunshine'** is an invaluable evergrey shrub, which is quick to establish and shoots back well after damage.

***Stephanandra incisa* 'Crispa'** is a very reliable, deciduous ground cover plant.

***Ulex europaeus*** (gorse) is very floriferous and tough; its dark green shoots and spines make it appear evergreen.

***Weigela*** varieties have profuse flowers in midsummer; the purple variety is more interesting than the common weigela.

## HERBACEOUS PLANTS

***Alchemilla mollis*** (lady's mantle) has attractive leaves and green-yellow flowers in midsummer. It recovers well if damaged by projectiles.

***Ballota pseudodictamnus*** is a white, woolly sub-shrub or perennial, with round, felted leaves. It does well in dry situations and grows up to 60cm (2ft).

***Bergenia*** varieties form a useful, bold-leaved, evergreen ground cover, and are fairly tough. Flowers are pink, white, red or purple according to variety.

***Euphorbia robbiae*** (spurge) is an attractive evergreen with showy, lime-green bracts. It can be invasive and grows to 60cm (2ft) high. The plants do best in semi-shade or shade.

***Geranium*** varieties. All the vigorous herbaceous geraniums (as opposed to the tender pelargoniums) are excellent, tough, colourful ground-cover plants. The foliage is neat and some varieties, for example *G. endressi* 'Wargrave Pink' are evergreen.

***Lamium*** (deadnettle). The less invasive *L. maculatum* 'Beacon Silver' and *L. m.* 'Chequers', are quick spreading, carpeting plants. They often have attractive marbled or variegated leaves and pretty pink, white or yellow flowers. Any damage is soon replaced by regrowth.

***Nepeta*** (catmint) has scented grey foliage and lavender blue flowers all summer. These are very common but deservedly so, as they are tough and easy to grow.

***Polygonum*** (knotgrass) includes some good, tough carpeters. *P. bistorta* 'Superbum' is an attractive plant, growing up to 75cm (2½ft) high, with large leaves and striking, light pink poker-shaped flowers for a two to three month period. Others are less dramatic but useful.

***Stachys byzantina*** (lamb's ears) is a familiar plant, loved by children for its furry, grey leaves. *S. b.* 'Sheila McQueen' has large grey-green leaves.

foliage always looked stunning. Some peonies are less sturdy, so choose yours carefully.

## ESTABLISHING PLANTS

Whatever you plant in a vulnerable position, allow it to establish itself before you let the children loose on it. A temporary fence of sticks and string, coupled with much discipline, may be necessary until the plants get going.

*In my own garden I have opted for a low box hedge to protect the more vulnerable plants such as penstemons and hardy osteospermums planted behind. This is the large box,* Buxus sempervirens, *which forms a decent barrier from cuttings in about three to four years.*

# Simple Plants for Children to Grow

The unfurling of new leaves and the blossoming of flowers can seem magical to a child, and the beauty of this is that it is so attainable; many plants can be grown in a small space on a balcony, or even a windowsill. As the children grow they can start to make a real contribution to the garden, and you will find that children will pick, wash and eat their own vegetables with gusto – even normally unpopular vegetables such as spinach.

## CHOOSING PLANTS

Younger children with a shorter concentration span should grow plants which will do something notable sooner rather than later. Avoid seeds that are prone to rot, have poor germination figures or need lots of heat – you may prefer to go for a safe bet initially and purchase small bedding or vegetable plants (though many vegetable seeds are easy to

*Buddlejas are an all-time favourite with children on account of the attraction they hold for butterflies. They do very well in containers, and this one has the added draw of an iguana decorating the side.*

grow). Courgettes are good value, with large yellow flowers that are slowly pushed off by the rapidly growing vegetables. Onions or shallots from sets are very easy, and are fun to string up afterwards. Lettuce, be it red or green, germinates very fast and is soon ready to eat.

Pelleted seed is much easier for small children to handle and so can be sown more precisely, although peas and beans have large seeds anyway and are quick to respond when sown. There are also many flowers which are easy to grow and have fairly large seeds, for example sweet peas, which can be sown outside in beds in early spring and trained up canes, or grown to form a hedge. Some old-fashioned Grandiflora types possess a wonderful overpowering fragrance, far better than the modern Spencer varieties. Pansies have a smaller seed, but are still manageable,

*Small children are riveted by water, and this little pool is on an ideal scale for a child to manage and enjoy. They can observe the life cycle of frogs, divide and replant aquatic plants such as water forget-me-knots, decorate areas with shells or hunt for watersnail eggs, learning as they play.*

*The children who are tending these cabbages have devised a harmless and attractive way to protect them from unwanted pigeons. These metallic cats, suspended from threads tied to sticks, have glistening eyes which move as they blow in the wind.*

Children enjoy embellishing and developing their plots. Encourage them by providing easy-to-grow, stunning plants which perform quickly, such as bedding plants on the point of flowering, so that their relatively short attention span does not become exhausted. Never force them to do tedious jobs but concentrate instead on making gardening fun.

and good results can be obtained for the spring and summer types by broadcasting them outside in early spring. These may take 2–3 weeks to germinate. Cornflowers sown in early spring will come up within a week, and can be broadcast in a mix with native poppies.

In late spring there are many suitable seeds for broadcasting in eye-catching spaces. *Nigella*, or love-in-a-mist, grows fast, has a reasonable-sized seed and is exquisite in flower. I prefer the all-blue 'Miss Jekyll' to the pastel mixes such as 'Persian Jewels Mixed' but children may well like variety. *Papaver nudicaule* (Iceland poppies) come in a colourful range of apricot, orange, yellow and scarlet

and look dramatic broadcast in patches in the border; they will take about two weeks to germinate. *Tropaeolum* (nasturtium), *Consolida* (larkspur), *Salvia*, *Helianthus* (sunflower), *Lavatera trimestris* (mallow) and *Calendula* (marigold) are all colourful, quick and easy too. Lupins are a striking perennial to grow; the hard seed case can be rubbed between two pieces of fine sandpaper to hasten germination.

Children enjoy doing things with their plants – admittedly not always the type of things one would expect. Plants such as pumpkins, runner beans, squashes and trailing nasturtiums are ideal, as they can fiddle with the stems and encourage them to climb up a

homemade wigwam or fence. With the nasturtiums they can also pick the small green seeds and help you pickle them – an ideal substitute for capers, and far less expensive.

### ORNAMENTAL BEDS

Brightly coloured vegetables such as the purple beetroot 'Bull's Blood', pink, white and green ornamental cabbages and red cut-and-come-again lettuce can be interspersed with some annual flowers to form growing letters, numbers, pictures and patterns, rather similar to (but possibly more interesting to children than) the traditional bedding patterns that are still seen in parks.

*ABOVE This fine hazel tunnel adorns a potager garden and provides an ideal structure for climbers. See right for how to make it.*

### HAZEL FRAMES

*RIGHT If you coppice hazel bushes they will throw up several straight shoots ideal for making wigwams, hurdles, tunnels, fences and so on. Cut the wood when it is still pliable and use it before it dries out. To make a tunnel you will need three long sticks, one for each side and one to connect the sides and form the top. Bind them together to keep the shape. Connect the arches with horizontal sticks to make the tunnel.*

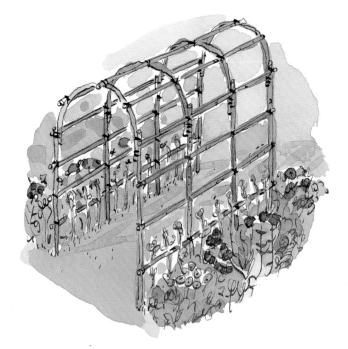

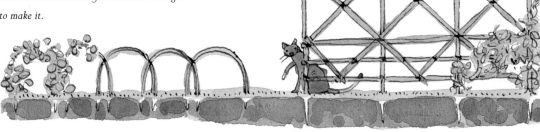

*LEFT Hazel fences are ideal boundaries around a child's plot. The hurdle fence is a useful and attractive way to demarcate areas of more precious planting or to discourage a young puppy. Many different variations of the lattice fence can be made, using hazel sticks bound with twine.*

### TREE SEEDS

Sowing seed is a surprisingly rapid way of establishing trees, though some seeds are slow to germinate, ash being one example. Oak seeds, conversely, may have already sent out roots before you have collected them. Other trees that are easy to grow are horse chestnut, beech, walnut, hazel, silver birch and alder.

In autumn, sow the freshly collected seeds individually at the same depth as their size in deep pots with about 2.5cm (1in) of free-draining material in the base and moist compost to just below the top. Your two main problems will probably be mice and rot, so cover your pots with a fine wire mesh and do not overwater, though the compost should be kept moist. When the weather warms up in spring, the seeds should start to sprout. The

*A selection of tree seedlings in pots decorate this spare corner, and the children have created a temporary garden with them. If seedlings do not germinate in the first year, just leave them for another year or two.*

seedling leaves (cotyledons) will be different from the true leaves, which will follow on quickly. As soon as the root system has a good hold, move the seedlings to their final position and water them well for the first month or so. If they are not ready to move out until summer, leave them until the autumn; any that do not germinate the first year can be left in situ for another year. Do not allow weeds or grass to compete with them for several years.

---

### ALNUS GLUTINOSA (COMMON ALDER)

*This bears male and female catkins on the same tree. The smaller female catkins form little cones. Collect these when they open, between autumn and early spring, and place on paper in a warm dry place. When they are dried shake out the seed and sow in moist compost, putting about 5–10 seeds in a pot as many are empty.*

### AESCULUS HIPPOCASTANUM (COMMON HORSE CHESTNUT)

*These large fruits are fun to collect and it is well worth reserving some for growing into trees. Remove the conkers from the outer green case, if necessary, and sow immediately after collection in early to mid-autumn, as soon as they are brown.*

### QUERCUS ROBUR (COMMON OAK)

*Collect acorns in early to mid-autumn, after the first frost. Remove the 'cups'. Soak the acorns overnight in warm water and then sow in compost in autumn or winter. Protect well against predators. Cover with an extra 7–10cm (3–4in) of compost and remove in early spring.*

### CORYLUS AVELLANA (HAZEL)

*Collect the nuts in autumn as soon as they are ripe, when the bracts (the papery cases which contain the nuts) start to turn brown. You need to be quick off the mark to gather them before the squirrels do. Remove the bracts and sow straight away with the hard shell intact. Protect the pots well, and make sure that they are exposed to 12–16 weeks of cold winter weather.*

### BETULA PENDULA (SILVER BIRCH)

*The smaller female catkins start to break up when ripe, dispersing tiny winged nutlets or 'seeds'. Collect the female catkins in autumn or winter and place on paper in a dry place. Collect the nutlets when the catkins fall apart and sow, 5–10 to each pot as some will be blind. Leave outside for four weeks when cold, then speed germination by bringing inside in early spring.*

### JUGLANS REGIA (COMMON WALNUT)

*Collect the nuts in autumn, as soon as the husks turn black, and the remove the husk. Soak them overnight in warm water. Sow the nuts in their shells straight away, covering them with 2.5–5cm (1–2in) of compost. Protect the pots from vermin and expose them to at least 12–16 weeks of cold weather.*

# Adventure Mazes

Mazes have a long history and a wide geographical distribution. Turf mazes, made by simply cutting patterns out of the turf, are thought to have been common in Britain in prehistoric times; in Scandinavia, ancient mazes formed from pebbles and large boulders, some of which would have required several men to carry them, have been discovered; some of the medieval churches in Europe incorporated a maze in an area paved with tiles, and the ancient Mediterranean world had its fair share too. The reasoning behind their construction is not known, but it is thought that the earliest ones had some significance in the initiation ceremonies of the Neolithic culture, helping to channel energy from the earth by means of a dance ritual acted out on the winding paths.

Today we are more familiar with the clipped hedge mazes often found in the gardens of historic homes and other major buildings. These have much more recent origins, the oldest in Britain being that at Hampton Court, which dates from about 1690. The hedge mazes, often fantastic in their size and complexity, were and are supposedly places for quiet contemplation, or more frequently for indulging in games of hide and seek or chase.

*LEFT Tunnels formed from willow cuttings are ideal for many games. You could make a labyrinth out of a whole system of tunnels which would bring a magical touch to your garden in about two growing seasons. It would cost next to nothing and everybody could have a hand in making it.*

## MAZES FOR ALL AGES

Mazes provide outdoor puzzles which fascinate all ages. The examples which decorate the spacious grounds around large country houses are often made with tall dark hedges of yew, beech, hornbeam or laurel, among which you could become thoroughly lost, while lower-growing mazes of dwarf hedges of hyssop, santolina, box or thyme form a delightful, often sweet-smelling, pattern which is immediately obvious. At a farm in Cambridgeshire, England there used to be a sunken maze with paths about 90cm (3ft) deep which children adored as they could hide in it or climb up over the sides. It drew them like a magnet and did not give that claustrophobic feeling engendered by the large hedge mazes.

Although many new large hedge mazes are being created in gardens open to the public,

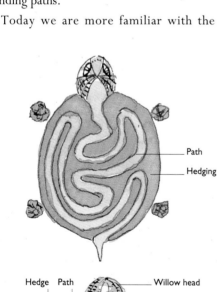

Path

Hedging

Hedge  Path  Willow head

Cross section

*A turtle has been created from a patternwork of low hedging such as box and narrow paths. His head is made of willow cuttings trained to form a tiny bower.*

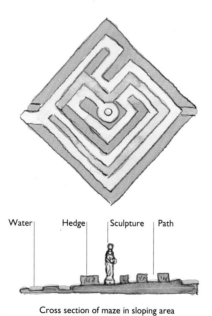

Water | Hedge | Sculpture | Path

Cross section of maze in sloping area

*This maze is formed from low clipped hedges, narrow paths and a rill of running water. A sculpture forms the centrepiece.*

**THE PLAN**
① Log stepping-
   stones
② Logs for playing
③ Weeping willow
④ Mini amphitheatre
⑤ Balancing posts
⑥ Willow tunnel
⑦ Teepee
⑧ Sandpit
⑨ Willow igloo
⑩ Pool
⑪ Boulders
⑫ Play fence and
   gate

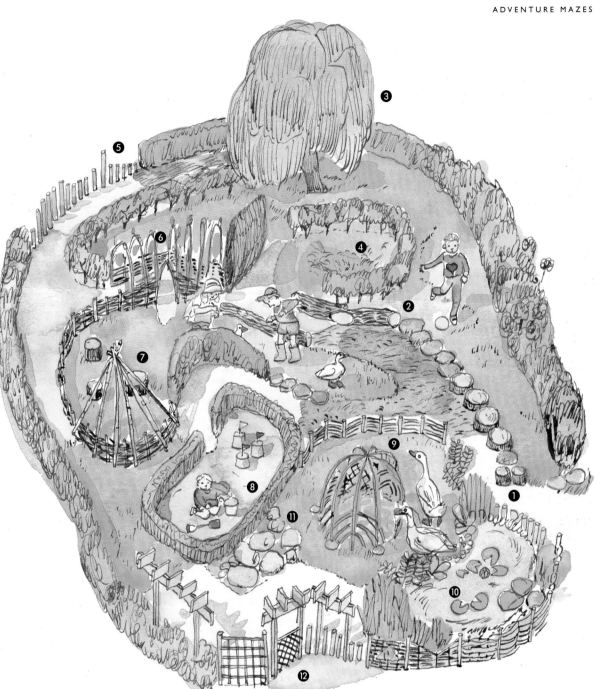

*RIGHT An adventure maze designed to encourage a wide range of play activities. All the elements are simple and inexpensive to construct, and they work well together as well as individually. Designed for an area of about 11 x 11m (36 x 36ft) the maze could be adapted to fit a much smaller space.*

not many people would want one in their own garden. On the other hand, a small pattern of lower, less imposing hedges leading to a central feature such as an arbour, seat or sundial can add a delightful element to a family garden. Laid out with tough dwarf hedges such as *Buxus sempervirens* or *Hebe anomala* and with a narrow path of gravel edged with brick, it can be used for gentle strolling or for games of chase. It need not take up more than a few square metres, and can be made to look quaint, charming and historical or modern and geo-

metric, depending on the materials you choose to use. A shallow channel of water, echoing the patterns of the pathway, would enhance both the relaxation and play value enormously.

**A ROUGH-AND-READY MAZE**
Alternatively, if you have a small patch going spare, a more rugged maze could form the centrepiece for children's activities in a wilder part of the garden. Make it in a rough-and-ready way out of materials you have to hand. The basic network can be cut out of the turf,

and different attractions can be sited in 'laybys' off the paths: a sunken sandpit surrounded by large boulders, a mounded area to make a miniature amphitheatre, a small weeping tree for a hideaway, willow arches, stepping-stone logs and drainpipe tunnels covered with climbers.

At his house in Kent, England, Charles Darwin laid a network of sandpaths around his garden. Here he would gently pace when he was trying to resolve an awkward question, kicking a stone each time he did a circuit.

# Topiary

The addition of some topiary to a garden can add a touch of grandeur, formality or fun, transforming even an ordinary garden into one that seems quite special. The job of clipping, shaping and growing it is soothing and quite absorbing, and if you get it wrong you can correct it next time round.

### CHOOSING THE PLANTS

Many plants can be used but the most common are *Laurus nobilis* (bay), *Fagus sylvatica* (beech), *Buxus sempervirens* (box), *Juniperus communis* (juniper), *Crataegus monogyna* (hawthorn), *Ilex aquifolium* (holly), *Carpinus betulus* (hornbeam), *Lonicera nitida*, *Ligustrum ovalifolium* (privet), and *Taxus baccata* (yew). Many garden centres are selling topiary specimens grown from fast-growing conifers such as *Cupressocyparis leylandii* (Leyland cypress), but although they make the grade much

quicker, the frequency of cutting they require invariably means that they are neglected sooner rather than later.

I favour box, because it roots extremely easily from 15cm (6in) heeled cuttings plunged straight into ordinary free-draining soil; by taking some cuttings each year you will soon build up a small nursery bed of different-sized plants to play around with. While the cuttings may take a year to root, the vast majority will

*BELOW LEFT Children will love creating a cat like this, and with a bit of help from an adult, it is quite feasible.*

*BELOW CENTRE Balls are one of the easiest shapes to form. Start with one, then let the central shoots grow on to form the next ball and so on.*

*BELOW RIGHT These squirrels form an amusing feature at the base of the steps. The addition of tubs is a good way of making topiary seem larger at an early stage.*

succeed, forming a good bushy plant ripe for titivation in three or four years. Topiary box is ideal in containers as it will tolerate lack of watering during periods of absence and will look eyecatching even during fairly lengthy periods of neglect.

### BEGINNING A SHAPE

When you start your topiary, try to go with the natural form of the plant as far as possible. You will find that simple geometric shapes are the easiest to start with, you can either do these by eye or use strings as a guide. If you go for a more complex shape you may need supports of canes and wire, but take care not to constrict the stems too much.

Ready-made frames are available for many superb shapes, and for children particularly I think they are well worth while as they give them an instantly pleasing form.

# PROJECT: A TOPIARY PEACOCK

For the impatient young (or old) gardener, buy a topiary wire frame of a peacock. Select a suitable variety of ivy – the best are those with small leaves, such as *Hedera helix* 'Glacier', which has small silvery-grey leaves, or *H. h.* 'Green Ripple', with small mid-green leaves. If you are keeping your peacock indoors, there is a large selection of more tender varieties to choose from too.

Plant two ivy plants in a 20–23cm (8–9in) pot with drainage crocks in the base. Assemble the frame according to the manufacturer's instructions, then tie the longest shoots to the tail and the shorter ones up the neck and head. Wrap any remaining shoots around the body. Carry on tying in new growth until the frame is completely covered, trimming regularly to keep in shape. Feed with a liquid fertilizer through the growing season and you should soon have a plump peacock.

Instead of ivy you could use *Buxus sempervirens* (box), *Rosmarinus officinalis* (rosemary) or *Lonicera nitida* (honeysuckle). The latter two are much faster, but would require regular trimming. Encourage children to use good children's scissors rather than secateurs, as they are much safer.

**❶** Plant two small-leaved ivies into a 20–23cm (8–9in) pot, then assemble and position the frame carefully around them.

**❷** Tie the longer shoots on to the tail, the shorter ones up the head and the remaining ones around the body.

*This fine specimen bird was assembled, planted, trained and trimmed up all in one growing season. He will, however, require regular tender loving care to keep him in such fine fettle. This involves clipping him frequently, watering and liquid feeding during the growing season and picking off dead leaves. He would make an ideal Christmas present and would be happy living indoors or out.*

# Children's Favourites

There are some plants that will keep younger children happy for hours, though they are not always ones the adults want to have around – such as dandelions, whose clocks can be blown around the garden to set seed in yet more places, and daisies, which can be woven into chains. Older children will probably still deign to play with these from time to time, but they will also enjoy plants they can actually do something with. 'Step-over' apples, which can be trained to form an edging around a plot as well as supplying fruit, give very good value. If you cannot buy them ready trained, ask for a one-year-old maiden on a M27 dwarf rootstock and cut back the leader to about 15cm (6in) above the graft. Then train out two shoots from the subsequent growth along a horizontal wire or cane about 30cm (12in) above the ground.

Strawberry plants in a strawberry pot are colourful and easy, and it is fun to help in-crease the quantity of fruit set by tickling the flowers with a small paintbrush. The fruits of cape gooseberry can be fun to collect when the pretty calyces, or lanterns, have changed from green to pale golden brown and made into delicious sweets by dipping into melted white chocolate.

If you can, allocate your children a small area of garden which is free from invasive weeds and has good, easy-to-work soil with a sunny aspect, and encourage them to grow some of the more child-friendly plants to kindle their gardening instincts. A diverse range of plants, varying the mix from year to year, will broaden their horizons, but until they are confident gardeners it is best to stick with easy-to-grow species.

*LEFT Strawberries are a hot favourite with many and a few strawberry plants in a pot or to grow in a patch of earth would be a much-appreciated present for a strawberry addict. Try to get some early fruit by protecting the plants with fleece or straw.*

*TOP RIGHT Grown in good light,* Dionaea muscipula *(Venus fly trap) often becomes deep red. Insects landing on the pads trigger them to close so the plant captures its prey. This is dissolved by enzymes to allow the nutrients to be absorbed.*

*CENTRE RIGHT* Physalis franchettii *(Chinese lantern) produces whitish-violet flowers in mid-summer, followed by orange-red fruit borne in an inflated bladder-like calyx which is up to 75mm (3in) long.*

*BOTTOM RIGHT A weeping willow with curtains of foliage forming a complete circle around the trunk provides a magnificent play space for young children. As the children grow they can climb the trunk, creating an upper storey to their den.*

# Plants of interest to children

## TREES

**Betula pendula 'Youngii' (weeping birch)** These small weeping birches quickly form small dens for younger children.

**Fraxinus excelsior 'Pendula' (weeping ash)** A more unusual weeping tree which will form a pleasing den.

**Malus domestica 'Ballerina' (orchard apple)** These trees grow on one vertical stem requiring little space and no pruning or stakes, crop heavily and quickly and can be grown in tubs.

**Malus domestica Step-over apples (orchard apple)** These trees are trained to form a low 'step over' fence, so make an ideal productive fence around a child's (or adult's) plot.

**Malus domestica Family apple (orchard apple)** These apple trees have several different varieties grafted on to one trunk, so are an ideal way to obtain more varieties of apples in a small space. They offer children a pleasing choice of which type of apple to pick from just one tree.

**Malus 'Golden Hornet' (crab apple)** A crab apple on the dwarfing rootstock M27 will form a tree no more than 1.5m (5ft) high, an ideal size for a child's tiny garden. It produces white flowers and bright yellow fruits.

**Prunus sp. (sweet cherry)** These are good trees for small treehouses, with excellent fringe benefits of blossom and cherries.

**Salix x 'Chrysocoma' (weeping willow)** My favourite plant when I was a child. Let the branches grow right down to the ground to form a thick, green curtain for a well-camouflaged den. This is for large gardens only – take care to plant well away from buildings, as the roots can have a devastating effect on foundations.

## SHRUBS, GRASSES, HERBACEOUS AND AQUATIC PLANTS

**Bamboos** The larger bamboos produce long canes which are useful for constructing dens, temporary fences and archways. The plants themselves can make ideal dens.

**Buddleja spp. (butterfly bush)** This shrub is often covered in butterflies. It will grow in poor, dry soils, so is a good plant for a container.

**Corylus avellana (cobnut)** Apart from the long yellow catkins, this shrub will provide wonderful wands for making archways, dens, fences and so on, with edible nuts as a further bonus. Try also the contorted form, *C. a.* 'Contorta', with its curious twisted branches.

**Dictamnus albus (burning bush)** A perennial plant that forms dense clumps and has pink or white flowers. The leaves are so highly aromatic that they can be set alight on hot, still, summer evenings and the gases will burn dramatically for a second or two – though this is obviously not a suitable trick for young children to perform.

**Digitalis purpurea (foxglove)** This easy, pretty plant has bold purple-spotted flowers which bumble bees favour. All parts of the plant are poisonous and the foliage can sometimes cause a skin reaction, but provided children are supervised and warned of the dangers it can be grown.

**Gunnera manicata** This huge-leaved perennial is an exotic plant to play in, although not ideal for younger children as it has spines on the leaf stalks. It likes a moist soil.

**Salix caprea (pussy willow)** This native willow will quickly grow to about 3m (9ft) tall and can be coppiced to keep it to that height. The furry silver catkins fascinate children. A small group of these could form the basis of a tough den.

**Stachys lanata (lamb's ears)** This useful ground-cover plant has soft woolly grey leaves which young children like stroking.

**Typha latifolia (bullrush)** A plant with fascinating cylindrical dark brown seedheads. However, it is too invasive for most garden pools, and *Typha angustifolia* is a better choice if yours is small.

## ANNUALS, SOFT FRUIT AND VEGETABLES

**Antirrhinum majus (snapdragon)** A particular favourite of children, who like to pinch the blossoms and make the 'dragon mouth' open and close.

**Fragaria x ananassa (strawberry)** Most children enjoy looking after their own strawberries as well as eating them. Strawberry planters which house several plants per pot are an interesting way to grow them.

**Cucurbita maxima (pumpkin)** Children can have great fun training these up stout canes and then making lanterns out of the massive mature fruits.

**Cucurbita pepo (ornamental gourd)** These are purely ornamental, but they are attractive and fun to grow.

**Helichrysum bracteatum (everlasting flowers)** The flowers of this plant are excellent for drying. When fresh they have a crisp texture, and come in bold colours.

**Helianthus annuus (common sunflower)** This rapid-growing giant-sized plant with magnificent brightly coloured flowers is a long-established favourite with children.

**Impatiens walleriana (busy Lizzie)** A prolific flowerer that can be brought into the house in the winter as a pot plant, and is easy to increase by means of cuttings.

**Lunaria annua (honesty, money plant)** The dried seedpods of this plant slightly resemble silver coins. The plant itself is delightful, with its soft purple flowers and its useful habit of self-seeding. The variegated form is wonderful.

**Mimosa pudica (sensitive plant)** Easily grown from seed, this plant has ferny foliage which folds together when touched. Grow as an annual in the garden or as a pot plant.

**Physalis franchetii (Chinese lantern)** This plant has bright orange papery lanterns enclosing a cherry-like berry, which is attractive in winter arrangements. It may be grown as a perennial or an annual.

**Physalis edulis (Cape gooseberry)** This has 'magic lanterns' enclosing the most delicious orange fruits which can be eaten raw, dipped in white chocolate or made into jam. A must for children.

## OTHER PLANTS

**Cacti** Children often have a cactus as their first plant. Many of these spiny plants take little looking after and occasionally produce stunning flowers.

**Dionaea muscipula (Venus flytrap)** This carnivorous plant is satisfyingly gruesome to watch as the traps (which become red in sunlight) catch a fly and slowly absorb it.

**Pleiospilos bolusii (living rock)** These small succulents grow in clumps exactly resembling stones and are an unusual plant for a child to grow indoors. They produce golden-yellow flowers in early autumn.

# Common Poisonous Plants

Plants are responsible for only a small proportion of accidents around the home, and these are rarely serious. However, it does pay to make it clear to children that they should not sample any plants except those that you have confirmed to be edible.

Apart from the list here of common toxic plants, there are many others which although not deadly can provoke severe reactions if certain parts are eaten. These include many widely grown garden plants such as anemone, aquilegia, arum, bryony, *Buxus* (box), *Hedera* (ivy), hellebore, juniper, kalmia, *Ligustrum* (privet), lobelia, lupin, clematis, *Convallaria majalis* (lily of the valley), daffodil, *Robinia pseudocacia* (false acacia), *Sambucus* (elder), foxglove, tomatoes, potatoes, *Rheum* (rhubarb), *Symphytum* (comfrey) and wisteria, to name a few. To exclude all these would be impractical: it is unlikely that a child would eat quantities of elder foliage, for example.

Even in the case of the plants in the Poisonous Plant Directory, I include *Taxus* (yew) and *Aconitum* (monkshood) in my garden. When children are too young to comprehend but old enough to be mobile – usually a short period – they are closely watched. Older children can understand that they should treat the plant with respect.

The majority of plants have not been tested for toxicity, so do not assume that any plants not described as toxic are necessarily harmless. Another aspect to bear in mind is that some plants can cause other injury – for instance, the tips of yucca leaves are often at the right height for a young child's eye, and rough-edged leaves, rose thorns and so on can also inflict a wound. Make sure that tetanus vaccinations are kept up to date.

If any of the plants described in the list opposite as severely toxic are eaten, you should seek urgent medical help from your doctor or an accident and emergency department. Take a sample of the plant with you, do not panic and do not make the patient sick.

*LEFT TO RIGHT Aconitum is charming but toxic; the splendid blooms of Datura are tempting but toxic; the spectacular Gloriosa superba might also attract; treat Heracleum mantegazzianum with respect; the poisonous seeds of Laburnum anagyroides could be picked up by young children; Ricinus communis can cause allergic reactions.*

## Poisonous Plant Directory

***Aconitum* spp. (monkshood)** All parts of the plant are severely toxic, especially the roots. The chemicals in the foliage cause skin irritation.

***Aethusa cynapium* (fool's parsley)** This common weed could be mistaken for parsley by a child. Its degree of toxicity is uncertain.

***Atropa belladonna* (deadly nightshade)** All parts of this native perennial are severely toxic, and the black berries may well be tempting to children.

***Conium maculatum* (hemlock)** All parts of this tall white flowering weed are severely toxic. The plant can also cause allergic skin reactions.

***Datura* spp. (angels' trumpets)** All parts of these plants are severely toxic.

***Euphorbia* spp. (spurge)** These widely grown plants are toxic if eaten, though not severely so. The more common problem is an allergic skin reaction which may occur in some individuals. Blisters, redness and itching may occur up to six days after contact.

***Gloriosa superba* (glory lily)** All parts of this stunning flowered deciduous climber are severely toxic if eaten, and the tubers will cause a skin reaction similar to a mild chemical burn, though this is unlikely to be serious or long-lasting.

***Heracleum mantegazzianum* (giant hogweed)** If eaten this spectacular plant is severely toxic. The commoner complaint is that when the sap comes in contact with the skin in strong sunlight it sensitizes it, causing bad sunburn, itching and burning followed by dramatic blisters. The damage to the skin may last for six months or more; the other effects wear off in a few weeks.

***Hyoscyamus niger* (henbane)** This unpleasant-smelling annual/biennial weed has dull creamy yellow, bell-shaped flowers with purple veins. It is common on bare and disturbed ground, particularly near the sea. All parts of the plant are severely toxic and can also cause skin irritation.

***Ipomoea* spp. (morning glory)** The seeds of these plants are severely toxic.

***Laburnum* spp.** All parts of these trees are severely toxic, especially the seeds which resemble peas in a pod.

***Colchicum* spp.** All parts of these spring- and autumn-flowering plants are severely toxic if eaten and may also cause a skin reaction.

***Daphne* spp.** All parts of all these popular evergreen and deciduous shrubs are severely toxic if eaten, especially the seeds. The sap may cause a skin reaction similar to a mild chemical burn, although this is unlikely to be serious or long-lasting.

***Nerium oleander* (oleander)** All parts of these evergreen shrubs are severely toxic if eaten. In addition, some people may have an allergic skin reaction to the foliage, though this is unusual.

***Nicotiana* spp. (tobacco plant)** These attractive plants are severely toxic if any part of them is eaten. They may be a hazard to animals.

***Ricinus communis* (castor-oil plant)** All parts of this bold-foliaged plant are severely toxic, especially the seed. Contact with the foliage can also cause an allergic reaction in some people, resulting in blistering, redness and itching.

***Ruta* spp. (rue)** All parts of this plant are toxic if eaten, though not life-threateningly so. The foliage can irritate the skin and make it excessively sensitive to sunlight, causing severe sunburn often with itching and blistering. The itching usually disappears within a week or two, but the skin may be marked for six months or even more. Avoid coming into contact with this plant in strong sun.

***Taxus* spp. (yew)** All parts of this plant are severely toxic if eaten, though children will be most attracted by the berries. As it is often used for hedges, animals are more at risk.

***Veratrum* spp.** All parts of these shade-loving perennials are severely toxic if eaten. It is thought that the foliage may cause a skin reaction.

## List of Suppliers and Useful Addresses

**Design**
Werner de Bock, Landplan Associates, Barnwell All Saints, Peterborough, PE8 5PW. Tel. 01832 272969

Honor Gibbs, EDA Design Associates, Rose Cottage, Hollington, Long Crendon, Aylesbury, Bucks, HP18 9EF. Tel. 01844 208418

Bunny Guinness, Sibberton Lodge, Thornhaugh, Wansford, Cambs, PE8 6NH. Tel. 01780 782518

**Design and Construction**
Peter Farrell, 49 Main Street, Woodnewton, Peterborough Cambs PE8 5EB. Tel. 01780 470066

Roger Storr Landscape Management, 4 Worple Way, Richmond, Surrey, TW10 6DF. Tel. 0181 948 2460

**Play equipment**
*Playhouse* (p.42 bottom right) Mathew Burt Splinter Group, Albany Workshops, Sherrington, Warminster, Wilts BA12 0SP. Tel. 01985 850996

*Playhouse on stilts* (p.34 top right) Hartland Limited, Unit 4, Manor Farm, Kingston Lisle, Wantage, Oxon OX12 9QL. Tel. 01367 820005

*Timber Climbing Frame* (pp.56-7) New England Gardens Ltd, 22 Middle Street, Ashcott, Somerset TA7 9QB. Tel. 01458 210821

*Play equipment* (p.25) TP Activity Toys available from stockists nationwide.

*Garden Games Equipment* John Jaques and Sons Ltd, Surrey. Available from stockists nationwide.

*Geotextile membrane* e.g. 'Terram' manufactured by Terram Ltd and widely available from builder merchants.

*Safety surfaces* Playbark available from Melcourt, Eight Bells House, Tetbury, Glos GL8 8JG. Tel. 01666 502711

*Safety swing seats* (pp.60, 62) Available from Wickstead Leisure Ltd, Digby Street, Kettering, Northants NN16 8YJ. Tel. 01536 517028

**Water Features and Irrigation**
*Irrigation units for pots* (p.90) from Tanker Irrigation, Plantasy Ltd, Birds Mill House, Broxburn, West Lothian, EH52 5PB. Tel. 01506 857411

*Paddling pool fittings* available from irrigation specialists: Hortech Systems Ltd, Hallgate, Holbeach, Spalding, Lincs. Tel. 01406 426513

*Sun bubble fountain* (p.115) and other water features designed and made by Jessica Slater, The Basement Studio, The Village Hall, Church Walk, Kingscliffe, Northants PE8 6XD. Tel. 01780 470570/470199

**Paving**
*Small paving units* (p.104 far left) Blanc de Bierges, Eastrea Road, Whittlesey, Peterborough, Cambs PE7 2AG. Tel. 01733 202566

**Bound Gravel**
Imag Ltd, 5-7 Mill Street, Congleton, Cheshire CW12 1AB. Tel. 01260 278810

**Sculpture**
*Pot with iguana* (p.154) available from Eamonn Moore, Unit 61, Trent Business Centre, Canal Street, Long Eaton, Nottingham NG10. Tel. 0115 972 2700

*Scarecrow* (p.130) available from Scarcity of Scarecrows, Polly Kettle, Oakland Cottage, Green Way Lane, Charlton Kings, Cheltenham, Glos. GL52 6LA. Tel. 01242 239071

**Barbecue**
Portable barbecue (p.92) available from major stockists and Wolf-Garden, Ross-on-Wye, Herefordshire, HR9 5NE. Tel. 01989 767600

**Buildings and Furniture**
*Child's metal bench* (p.100) available from The General Trading Company, 144 Sloane Street, London SW1X 9BL. Tel. 0171 730 0411

*Indian building* (p.104 far left) from Andrew Crace Designs, Bourne Lane, Much Hadham, Herts, SG10 6ER. Tel. 01279 842685

*Seat* (p.101 below) available from Nick Hodges, The Old Workshops, Church Walk, Wroxton, Banbury, Oxon OX15 6QF. Tel. 01295 730362

*Swing seat* (p.23 bottom) available from The Missenden Trading Co, 26 High Street, Great Missenden, Bucks HP16 9AB. Tel. 01494 890690

**Pets**
Information available from: The Pet Health Council, Thistledome Cottage, 49 Main Street, Sewstern, Grantham, Lincs NG33 5RF. Tel. 01476 861379

**Topiary Frames** (p.161) Capital Garden Products, Gibbs Reed Barn, Ticehurst, East Sussex TN5 7HE. Tel. 01580 201092

The Wadham Trading Company, Wadham House, Southrop, Nr Lechlade, Gloucestershire GL7 3PB. Tel. 01367 850499

## Acknowledgements

Firstly, I would like to thank my own family, my husband, Kevin, and my children, Unity and Freddie for all their invaluable help and inspiration, without which this book would never have materialized.

I would also like to thank Anna Mumford of David & Charles for her help and support in making this book possible; the Art Editor, Lisa Tai, for her creativity, perserverance and unstinting hard work; Mike Trier for his input on the construction details; Juliette Wade for the superb photography and Kevin Hart for his excellent illustrations.

Grateful thanks are also due to Stefan Wrobel for his imaginative contributions and much hard work in producing several of the plans and drawings.

For the technical aspects, I would like to thank Rob Davies, Chief Engineer at Wickstead Leisure Ltd, Kettering, Northants for his advice on general construction details for play equipment and Anthony Blaine, John Simms and Peter Farrell for their advice on several of the construction details.

Thanks are also due to all those in the horticultural industry I have contacted while writing this book who have, without exception, been extremely generous with their time and knowledge. I would particularly like to mention Margaret and Martyn Handley of Dingle Plants and Gardens, Pilsgate, Stamford for their generosity in providing a wide variety of wonderful plants.

I am indebted to the children who appeared in the photographs, especially William Clayton, Rory and Esme Farrell, Victoria Fox, Unity and Freddie Guinness, Andrew and David Mobbs, Alison Rea, the Sands children, Preeya and Arun Takhar and Thomas and Sarah Williams.

Finally, I am grateful to the following people for allowing us to photograph their gardens: Mr and Mrs J. Arlsford, David and Pat Austin, Chris and Jill Barnes, Peter and Ann Barnet, Mrs Susan Brooke, Mr and Mrs J. Conant, Chris and Janet Cottam, Graham and Heather Coulter, Mr and Mrs S. Dale, Werner and Jan de Bock, John and Anne Denning, Mr and Mrs Darby Dennis, Mrs Jane Dyer, Mr. R. Edwards, Peter and Suzy Farrell, Mrs Helen Fickling, Prince and Princess Galitzine, Dr and Mrs Garton, Will Giles, Lady Gibberd, Barry and Honor Gibbs, Mrs Phillipa Gordon, Mrs Julia Greene, Sally Greene, Mr and Mrs Ian Hodgson, Mr and Mrs Norman Hudson, Phillip and Francesca Kendall, Mr. E. Lloyd, Mrs Mogford, Mr David Moisey, John and Fiona Owen, David and Jennifer Powell, Mr and Mrs Ratcliffe, Mr and Mrs J. Reynolds, Mr and Mrs S. Riley-Smith, The Roald Dahl Foundation, Sancton Wood Junior School, Mr and Mrs Sands, John and Emma Simms-Hilditch, Andrew and Jessica Slater, Phillip and Barbara Stockitt, Sheila and Roger Storr, Mr and Mrs R. Swallow, Mrs Worsick, Wyevale Garden Centres

**Picture acknowledgements**
Chris Baines pp.126 (top right), 135, 141 (top); Blanc de Bierges p.104 (far left); Matthew Burt Splinter Group p.42; Bunny Guinness pp.66 (bottom), 130, 137 (centre); Garden Picture Library: GPL/Brian Carter p.165 (right) GPL/Densy Clyne p.164 (right) GPL/Ron Evans p.162 (centre right) GPL/Sunniva Harte p.134 (left and right) GPL/Michael Howes p.162 (bottom right) GPL/John Glover p.164 (centre) GPL/Mayer & le Scanff p.127 (top) GPL/Howard Rice pp.164 (left), 165 (centre) GPL/J.S. Sira p.127 (bottom) GPL/Brigitte Thomas p.162 (top right); Nigel Temple p.44 (bottom); Steven Wooster pp.28, 29 (both), 67, 74 (bottom); Stefan Wrobel pp.40 (both), 45, 77, 115 (top left), 131 (top), 158 (top)

# Index

*Italic* page numbers refer to
picture captions.